The Coming Worldwide Calvary

The Coming Worldwide Calvary

Christ Versus Antichrist

DESMOND FORD

iUniverse, Inc.
New York   Bloomington

The Coming Worldwide Calvary
Christ Versus Antichrist

Copyright © 2009 Desmond Ford

iUniverse books may be ordered through booksellers or by contacting:

iUniverse
1663 Liberty Drive
Bloomington, IN 47403
www.iuniverse.com
1-800-Authors (1-800-288-4677)

ISBN: 978-1-4401-7284-7 (pbk)
ISBN: 978-1-4401-7285-4 (ebk)

Printed in the United States of America

iUniverse rev. date: 9/22/2009

Table of Contents

Introduction

We live in a troubled world. Science has not turned it into a Paradise. Neither have secularism nor humanism helped. More often parts of the globe seem like hell. Violence, corruption, impurity, blasphemy, theft, mendacity, and covetousness prevail in every land. They exist in the very forces appointed to control such evils—the state and the church.

"Is there any word from the Lord?" remains an appropriate question. If God is rational he can make a revelation of truth to his children, and if he is moral he must do so. Long ago, there visited our planet a God-man who in three-and-a-half years did much more than Socrates, Plato, and Aristotle in their combined 130 years. He alone ignored the trivial, the false, and the temporary and offered only that which is universal and eternal. That he was God's chief revelation is made sure by his prescience when he foretold that as long as sun, moon, and stars remain, his truth would be taught and believed. See Matthew 24:35. No one else among the ten billion who have lived on this planet ever said that.

When his disciples asked him for a sign that the end of the world was near, he gave it. "When you see the abomination of desolation spoken of by Daniel the prophet, then…" (Matthew 24:15). He said this sign would launch a time of tribulation worse than anything the world had ever known.

It is vital to notice that in the preceding verse he foretold that his good news would go to all the world just before these things took place. Therefore it is a mark of sanity to be concerned about understanding what these things are—the abomination of desolation, the gospel, and the tribulation. The explanation of these things is the purpose of this little book.

The first six chapters of this book are more demanding, but after that, the chapters are easy to read.

PART ONE

What Is the Abomination of Desolation?

Chapter One

What Is Coming?

Some form of infidelity and impiety will be established by Law in the Christian Church, as our Lord himself foretells (Matt. 24:15); as a heathen altar was set up by Antiochus Epiphanes in the temple at Jerusalem….

So will it be at the last times. The church itself will be betrayed by some in high places in her ministry, and by means of their timid and treacherous concessions and compromises it will be polluted by a form of worship which will make it execrable in the sight of God, and will cause all good men to weep and hide their faces in shame and sorrow.

Bishop Christopher Wordsworth, *Commentary on the Holy Bible*, Vol. 6, p. 62

We encounter "the abomination of desolation" in Daniel in passages dealing with persecution and oppression. … It seems probable that the symbol in question refers to some form of blasphemy which will characterize the last days.… Devastation will be … associated with it.

Lars Hartman, "Prophecy Interpreted," *Coniectanea Biblica*, New Testament Series, Vol.1, p. 152

The "abomination of desolation" is a formula indicating an overthrow of God's religion, a desecration of what is holy, and a dissipation and corruption of his order of worship by some great God-opposing power. This description is evidently applicable with more or less exactness to several crises in history including … Antichrist.

Joseph Tanner, *Daniel and the Revelation*, p. 56

> The abomination of desolation in the holy place, demanding worship and reverence, glorified by false prophets through word and miracle—that is the last great temptation…. This is the last and final catastrophe in history that Jesus sees coming. He was certain that the kingdom of God comes through suffering and only through suffering.
>
> J. Jeremias, *New Testament Theology,* vol. 1, pp. 128-29

"The abomination is the Antichrist described in 2 Thess. 2:4" (Jerome).

Note the following Scriptures: "Upon the earth distress of nations with perplexity" … "There will be great tribulation such as has not been from the beginning of the world…." "And if those days had not been shortened, no human being would be saved." "There shall be a time of trouble such as never has been since there was a nation." "Great distress shall be upon the earth … men fainting with fear and foreboding of what is coming on the world." "So when you see standing in the holy place 'the abomination that causes desolation' spoken of through the prophet Daniel—let the reader understand—then … flee."

> Immediately after the distress of those days the sun will be darkened and the moon will not give its light; the stars will fall from the sky, and the heavenly bodies will be shaken. At that time the sign of the Son of Man will appear in the sky, and all the nations of the earth will mourn. They will see the Son of Man coming on the clouds of the sky, with power and great glory. And he will send his angels with a loud trumpet call, and they will gather his elect from the four winds, from one end of the heavens to the other.
>
> Seventy sevens are decreed … to finish transgression, to put an end to sin, to atone for wickedness, to bring in everlasting righteousness, to seal up vision and prophecy and to anoint the most holy. … The end will come like a flood: War will continue until the end and desolations have been decreed.
>
> And I will give power to my two witnesses and they will prophesy 1,260 days, clothed in sackcloth…. now when they have finished their testimony, the beast that comes up from the Abyss will attack them, and overpower and kill them … but after the three and a half

days a breath of life from God entered them and they stood on their feet, and terror struck those who saw them.

The nations were angry; and your wrath has come. The time has come for judging the dead, and for rewarding your servants the prophets … and for destroying those who destroy the earth.

How long will it be before these astonishing things shall be fulfilled? The man clothed in linen … lifted his right hand toward heaven, and I heard him swear by him who lives forever, saying … when the power of the holy people has been finally broken, all these things will be completed."

But at that time your people—everyone whose name is found written in the book—will be delivered. Multitudes who sleep in the dust of the earth will awake: some to everlasting life, others to shame and everlasting contempt. Those who are wise will shine like the brightness of the firmament, and those who lead many to righteousness, like the stars for ever and ever.

When he opened the fifth seal, I saw under the altar the souls of them who had been slain because of the word of God and the testimony they had maintained. They called out in a loud voice, "How long, Sovereign Lord, holy and true, until you judge the inhabitants of the earth and avenge our blood?" They were told to wait a little longer, until the number of their fellow servants and brothers who were to be killed as they had been was completed.

He was given power to make war with the saints and to conquer them…. All inhabitants of the earth shall worship the beast—all whose names have not been written in the book of life. … All who refused to worship the image to be killed. … No one could buy or sell unless he had the mark…."

Then I saw another angel flying in midair, and he had the eternal gospel to proclaim to those who live on the earth—to every nation, tribe, language and people….

If anyone worships the beast and his image and receives his mark … he too will drink of the wine of God's fury which has been poured full strength into the cup of his wrath.

Then the dragon was enraged at the woman and went to make war with the rest of her offspring—those who obey God's commandments and hold to the testimony of Jesus.

Mystery
Babylon the Great.
The mother of prostitutes
And of the abominations of the earth.

I saw that the woman was drunk with the blood of the saints.

The beast and the ten horns you saw will hate the prostitute. They will bring her to ruin and leave her naked; they will eat her flesh and burn her with fire. For God has put it into their hearts to accomplish his purpose by agreeing to give the beast their power to rule until God's words are fulfilled. The woman you saw is the great city that rules over the kings of the earth.

In her was found the blood of prophets and of the saints, and of all who have been killed upon the earth.

And I saw the souls of those who had been beheaded because of their testimony for Jesus and because of the word of God. They had not worshipped the beast or his image and had not received his mark…. They came to life and reigned with Christ a thousand years.

The foregoing offers samples from Scripture about the great distress unequalled from the beginning of the world (Matthew 24:21) soon to overtake our globe. It will not come without warning, and it is the purpose of this book to explain that warning and the contexts that enshrine it. Because the great distress is immediately preceded by the proclamation of the true authentic gospel to all on earth, this study will explain the nature and content of that gospel. It will also unveil prevalent false gospels.

No one can read the Olivet discourse, or the books of Daniel and Revelation, without becoming aware that a great crisis awaits the earth and the people of God. Passion Week is to be repeated on a worldwide scale with the body of Christ persecuted and suffering as he once did. The saints of the last days will be given power to proclaim the everlasting gospel to the whole world but the result will be anger and the threat of death ultimately fulfilled upon many.

The period of "prophesying in sackcloth" amidst threats and stresses will be succeeded by the shattering of the church. Then Christ will return to claim survivors and punish their persecutors, and raise the righteous dead.

The glorious promises of Daniel 9:24 (without parallel in the rest of Scripture) were fulfilled legally at Calvary, but their practical, empirical implementation will take place only after another Calvary—one worldwide, involving those who, like Christ at his triumphant entry, have given the gospel call, polarising the world.

There is to be an apocalyptic sign warning believers when the crisis is at hand. Antichrist in his final form, the ultimate abomination that causes desolation, will dominate the professed apostate church and issue his (or its) mandates of death. While the approach of the Roman armies against Jerusalem in A.D. 70 was the initial fulfilment of this prophecy (Mark 13:14 and Matthew 24:15), the ultimate fulfilment, which will unveil Antichrist, is yet to come.

Here is the one prophecy of the Old Testament upon which Christ put his finger and commanded, "Understand it." But it is a complete mystery to most who claim to be Christ's, and not one in a thousand is endeavouring to fulfil the Saviour's command to understand Daniel's warning. This little book is an endeavour to take the Lord's admonition seriously and is the result of thousands of hours of study. That, of course, does not by itself guarantee infallibility, but it may tempt some to read and study the issues here raised.

"Blessed is he that reads."

Chapter Two

Daniel and the Last Sign

The desolating abomination, which one day will constitute the final sign of the end, is typified throughout the early pages of Daniel by persecuting kings, and it is then portrayed in visionary form in chapters 7 to 12—the prophecies of the book. When we recall that the book of Daniel had more influence upon the New Testament than any other book of the Old Testament its importance is verified. All of the eschatological teachings of Christ, the kingdom of God, the Son of man, the abomination of desolation, the last great tribulation, the judgment, and the resurrection—all have their origin here and are endorsed by the Savior. We cannot fully comprehend the teaching of Christ without a prior understanding of the ancient prophet.

The abomination of desolation is referred to in Daniel 8:13; 9:27; 11:31, and 12:11. Almost all commentators for over 2,000 years have recognized that the first fulfilment of this symbol was Antiochus Epiphanes, King of Syria, the first persecutor of the Jews who wished to annihilate them for religious reasons. (See my *In the Heart of Daniel*, page 105ff. and *Daniel and the Coming King*, pp. 231ff.). From 171 B.C. to 165 B.C., Antiochus waged war on Israel, desolating her sanctuary by the erection of a profane altar and idol. Forty thousand Jews perished in one onslaught, and a similar number were sold into slavery. The clearest description of what happened is found in the Apocrypha—a collection of uninspired Jewish books written between the time of Malachi and the coming of Christ. Note a portion of the history from First Maccabees.

> And king Antiochus wrote to his whole kingdom, that all should be one people, and that each should forsake his own laws. ... Many of Israel consented to his worship and sacrificed to the idols, and profaned the Sabbath. ... They built an abomination of desolation upon the altar ... and they rent in pieces the books of the law which they found, and set them on fire. And wheresoever was found with

any book of the covenant, ... the king's sentence delivered him to death ... and on the five and twentieth day of the month they sacrificed upon the idol altar, which was upon the altar of God. And the women that had circumcised their children they put to death ... and they hanged their babes about their necks, and destroyed their houses, and them that circumcised them.

1 Maccabees 1 (see also chapter 4)

For over a century it was customary for many Bible scholars to place Daniel in the second century B.C., rather than the time of authorship it claims—the sixth century B.C. Fortunately, the arguments used to support this position have been largely decimated in recent years. See the discussion of this topic in my books *In the Heart of Daniel* and in *Daniel and the Coming King.*

Like its twin, the New Testament book of Revelation, Daniel has been written with minute care and enshrines untold depths of truth for believers of these days. Daniel himself is a remarkable type of Christ—a prince of the house of Judah, exiled from home. No sin is recorded against him. Jealous rulers place him in a sealed death pit, but he is delivered. He intercedes in prayer at the Calvary hour for his sinful people, whom he loves without reserve and takes their guilt upon himself. And God hears his prayers and sends a comforting angel. The victorious Cyrus gives permission for Israel to return to her own land. This redemption in the book of Isaiah is used as a symbol of the greater redemption from sin's captivity. The antitypical Cyrus, who is Christ our Lord, achieves this.

The name Daniel means God is Judge, and every chapter of this book speaks of judgment and vindication. Righteousness is shown to triumph over transgression, sin, and iniquity. Finally, it is promised that everlasting righteousness will be brought in by the Messiah who, though murdered by those he came to save, will triumph over death as the Representative of his people. One day many will duplicate his final experience on earth before his resurrection.

A key word of the book is "deliver" (KJV), or "rescue" (NIV). See chapters 3, 6, and 12. The Old Testament saints of Daniel's day are threatened with death if they will not worship the way of dictators, but God delivers a faithful remnant. All this is shown by the prophecies to be typical of the way God will deliver the last generation of martyrs—though it may be from the grave itself.

Beginning with the very first verse, this ancient book depicts the representatives of evil violating God's way of worship, and enforcing their own. In chapter one the sacred temple is attacked and rifled. In chapter three its Decalogue is violated. In chapter five the sacred vessels of the sanctuary are profaned, and judgment falls upon the violators. The prophecies tell the same story. In chapter seven the little-horn figure of Antichrist in his various forms and eras, seeks to change the sacred times and the laws of God and "wears out" those who are loyal to God. In chapter eight the same power casts the temple, its services, and its truth to the ground, and the worshippers are martyred. In chapter nine the great Deliverer and his atoning death are foretold, making it impossible for him any longer to protect the Temple and its worshippers from Satan's attacks. The Temple and the city of Jerusalem are destroyed, but ultimately the abominable power that desolates is also brought to its end. Chapters 10 to 12 enlarge some of these features, and the wicked desolating power is referred to repeatedly in chapters 11 and 12.

About 30 times the words signifying "understand" are found in this book. Christ selected that key word when he referred to Daniel in his Olivet Discourse. It is those who "understand" who turn many to righteousness (Daniel 12:3), and they will shine like the stars for ever and ever. But it takes much searching, much "running to and fro" through the pages of Scripture to understand these vital matters (Daniel 12:4). This searching we will now endeavour to do.

Chapter seven of Daniel is the first to give visionary representation of Antichrist—a "little horn" that grows up among the 10 horns of the fourth terrible beast. It represents humanity making itself God, but in the same chapter, as the counterpart sign, we have one called the Son of man—deity making itself man. Here we see humility versus pride, meekness versus violence, truth versus error, and true worship versus idolatry. The Jews, before their conquest by Rome, interpreted the fourth beast of this prophecy as the Syrian portion of Alexander's empire, and the little horn, its king, as Antiochus Epiphanes. Much later they saw that the Roman Empire was a better (larger and more devastating) fulfilment. The Reformers saw also here a prediction of Christian apostasy after the fall of Rome, and a final Antichrist.

Chapter eight enlarges the antichrist theme and deserves our close attention. It is significant for many important reasons. Here are some of them:

1. It sets forth in miniature the great controversy between Christ and Satan over the whole range of time. The little horn in this prophecy is the same little horn of chapter seven (compare the characteristics given in the two chapters) and had its first fulfilment in the Old Testament antichrist, Antiochus Epiphanes—the first ruler who endeavored to extirpate God's people for religious reasons. But the symbol embraces other fulfilments such as pagan and spiritual Rome and the final Antichrist. Most of all it is a reflection of Satan, its great original and author. Revelation 12 makes that very plain as it repeats some of the symbolism of Daniel 8. The same chapter shows that Satan is the model Antichrist.

2. For the first time in prophecy we see angels curious as to the significance of the visionary drama. First Peter 1:10-12 refers to this chapter and tells us that it is about the sufferings of Christ and his subsequent glory. Christ is "the prince of the host," and "the prince of princes" referred to here, and the daily morning and evening burnt offerings mentioned are symbols of Christ's everlasting gospel. The Jews referred to them as "the continual," for they pointed to the influence of the Atonement over ceaseless ages. The sanctuary is an emblem of the church and of the kingdom of God.

3. It was Christ himself who came down to give light on the meaning of this vision. Calvin, Bishop Wordsworth, and other scholars have concluded that the "angel" who gave the message of verse 14 was none other than the Second Person of the Godhead. When the KJV scholars put in the margin adjoining verse 13 "the numberer of secrets, or the wonderful numberer," they had Christ in mind. The One who commanded Gabriel to give Daniel understanding was clearly Gabriel's superior. At the close of the book the august appearance of one who hovered over the waters (12:6-7) tells us that it was a divine being who supervised these visions. Compare Daniel 10:5-6 with Revelation 1:13-15. See also Psalm 93 and Matthew 8:23-27.

4. For the first time we read of "the time of the end," an expression which is always used eschatologically, according to R. H. Charles, and refers to the advent of the kingdom of God.

5. While for the first time in the book we are here told that Daniel could not understand this revelation, a later chapter assures us that in the last days "knowledge shall increase" as many run to and fro (a Hebraism for "searching") through these pages seeking for light. In our day Daniel can be understood as never before.

6. It was specifically to this prophecy and its later enlargements in the same book that Christ pointed and admonished all his followers to "understand."

7. Verse 14 of this chapter is the close of the symbolic portions of Daniel. After this all is explanation.

8. This chapter is the seedplot for all the remaining chapters of the book, and for all New Testament eschatology. Compare Daniel 8:13 with Matthew 24:15; 2 Thessalonians 2:3-4; and Revelation 11:2.

9. This chapter contains the key verse of the book (verse 14), the only one that uses the Hebrew term for "vindication," and vindication is the theme of each chapter of Daniel. Its emblem is "the Son of Man" in chapter seven, and this phrase is used 88 times in the New Testament with the same meaning. Daniel 8:14 is not explained in the following interpretation given by the angel, but it is explained in a later vision as recorded in Daniel 9:24-27. At the return of Christ, all God's ways are vindicated, and angels and humans will unite in singing, "Just and true are your ways, O King of the ages" (Revelation 15:3).

In studying this chapter we must remember that it is apocalyptic (using bizarre symbols associated with the end times), and that it both parallels its predecessors, chapters 2 and 7 (except for Babylon, because that kingdom had fallen), and the later chapters 10-12. Apocalyptic visions have cosmic range and do not have only a localized application.

Comparing this prophecy with the earlier and later ones, we find that Daniel 2:44-45; 7:13-14, 8:14; 9:24 and 12:13 are speaking of the same reality and complement each other.

The expression "transgression of desolation" ("the rebellion that causes desolation," NIV) is the equivalent of "the abomination of desolation" used in chapters 9, 11, and 12. The word translated "transgression" or "rebellion" signifies the height of apostasy, but the Hebrew term for "abomination" is used later because it signifies idolatry so bad that it emits a horrible stench. When the letters for the Hebrew term for "abomination" are given their Hebrew numerical equivalents, they total 490, reminding us that the prophecy of Daniel 9:24-27 about the "seventy sevens" is a prophecy of the grand jubilee symbolized by the number for perfection and completion multiplied by another symbolic number—70. Thus the consummation of the eternal kingdom of God ushered in by Christ's Second Advent is imaged, as well as its inauguration at Calvary.

In the nineteenth century, beginning with Baptist William Miller, many earnest Christians studying this chapter concluded it extended to the year 1844 and Christ's return. Because few of them knew anything about Hebrew, they were unaware that the word "days" is not in the original, nor is "cleansed." Therefore attempts to use the year-day principle (a traditional but non-biblical method of interpretation) and the type of Leviticus 16, where the sanctuary was cleansed, were actually invalid. Nevertheless God used this great awakening to challenge the popular postmillennial views of the time, and the message was attended by the witnessing power of the Holy Spirit. The doctrine of the Investigative Judgment was the fifth and last attempt of Adventists to explain the great disappointment. But here again they missed an obvious meaning of Daniel 8:14. That verse was the answer to the question as to how long the little horn would triumph. As in Daniel chapter seven, the villain—the little horn—is the subject of God's investigation, not faithful believers. All apocalyptic encourages the faithful and threatens the wicked.

There are depths in these prophecies not immediately apparent. For example, most Bible readers have seen Daniel 9:24 as applying to Christ's atonement at Calvary, but missed seeing that its apotelesmatic significance fits the end of the world—when that which has been accomplished legally becomes empirical reality. The last verses of the prophecy tell of the "cutting off" of the Messiah, his confirming of the covenant, and making sacrifice and offering to cease, as well as the pouring out of divine wrath upon Antichrist's final manifestation as the "abomination that causes desolation."

Not only does verse 24 have an eschatological meaning—the same is true of the verses just quoted. The body of Christ also is to be "cut off" by legal mandate and bloody persecution in the last days. But Christ will fulfil all the divine promises and enable his people (anointed by the Holy Spirit) to proclaim the gospel with power before their partial annihilation. This will be done "in sackcloth"—deep humiliation. They will have their own awful Calvary, yet witnessing to their oppressors. See Revelation 11:3. Then, when his own have met their martyrdom, he will cause his divine intercessions in the heavenly sanctuary to cease, and probation will close. At that point, no longer will the impenitent be protected by Christ's intercession. Then fall the terrible seven last plagues decreed for the destruction of Antichrist and his empire and people. And after that—glory!—the glory of the resurrection, and the new heavens and the new earth where sorrow is no more and death has fled away. So the everlasting covenant is confirmed for eternity, and sacrifice is ended. For a detailed explanation of Daniel 9:24-27, read *In the Heart of Daniel*.

Chapter Three

The Abomination of Desolation That Violates the Law from Sinai[1]

William Barclay wrote: "No one quite knows what the desolating abomination is." And the well-known *Pulpit Commentary* affirms that, "What is meant by the term is a matter of unsettled dispute." Certainly the phrase in many ways is the most mysterious in all literature. And yet Jesus assumes, not only that we CAN know, but that we MUST know the identity of this manifestation. He declares it is the chief sign of the approaching end of the world. He knew the prophecies about the abomination had been fulfilled 16 decades earlier, but now he applies them to a future climactic fulfilment.

When the disciples asked him what would be the sign of the end, he warned them not to take wars, earthquakes, or other natural phenomena as the sought after sign. Be not troubled, said Jesus, when these things take place—even persecution. BUT when you see the abomination of desolation ... then FLEE, for the greatest tribulation the world has ever known is approaching, and marks the very eve of the Last Judgment. The mysterious cryptogram from the prophecies of Daniel "tells more than a thousand words." While first fulfilled in A.D. 70, its final application now approaches.

Do not miss the conjunction of verses 14 and 15 in Matthew 24. The final manifestation of Antichrist will not only violate the law of God, but it will counterfeit the true gospel predicted in verse 14. And most of the world will be deceived. What are the key elements in the biblical contexts of "the abomination of desolation"? In our answer we must include the host trodden

---

[1]   By the law from Sinai we mean the original Edenic law of love to God and man, reaffirmed in the moral elements of the Mosaic Code, particularly, but not solely, given in Exodus 20. That code, as interpreted by the New Testament, remains God's guide for his children.

underfoot, the temple cast down, the victorious Antichrist figure, the righteous remnant who vindicate Yahweh, the vindication of holiness including the sanctuary and its worshippers, and the final deliverance coinciding with the destruction of the enemy and the establishment of the kingdom. Our phrase is not allied to petty themes but rather to ones of absorbing interest and importance, including such facets of the holy war as the Antichrist, the Remnant, Armageddon, the kingdom of God, and everlasting righteousness. The warning of Matthew 24:15 deals with the eternal controversy between right and wrong. Jesus points to the climax of this controversy. Believers should not be content with mere intellectual comprehension of the prophetic forecasts. The real test is whether our head, heart, and hands are in such harmony with the known will of God that we will survive the final Calvary.

The chronological setting for the phrase is Passion Week and the crisis reached by Judaism as a result of its unfaithfulness. The literary setting includes the chain of woes uttered against the leaders of the people. Beginning with the Triumphal Entry, all Christ's acts and words mirror the theme of impending judgment. Finally he declares "Your house is left unto you desolate." The ensuing discourse can only be understood properly when this framework is taken into account.

In effect, Mark 13 represents Christ as saying to the new Israel of God: "Because of the spiritual idolatry and apostasy of Israel's priests and teachers, a tragedy of even greater dimensions than those under Babylon and Syria awaits this rebellious people. As the sign of religious privilege, the Temple was then profaned and devastated (even as it must be in the near future). Be faithful; do not let your worship become tarnished as theirs was. Endure to the end, as did Daniel and his fellows, and the Maccabean heroes who were upright despite prevailing apostasy. Then you will be delivered from the fate impending for all those who, while professing godliness, are actually idolaters at heart."

Scholars have pointed out that Passion Week both casts light upon and is illustrated by Mark 13, the discourse that enshrines the abomination. The apostasy, which would lead to believers being hauled before kings and judges, and the tribulation prior to their exaltation, are akin to Christ's own experience after the apostasy of Judas. The Body is, of course, to share the vicissitudes of the Head. Christ expects desolation in body and spirit as a result of the apostasy of others, therefore let the church also be prepared for similar experiences and doubly aware lest they merit the same. Supporting this reality that the church will duplicate his experience and that Calvary awaits true believers, note the key words found in Christ's discourse about the future—"Watch," "betray," and "hour"—which also occur repeatedly in the following chapters as the Passion unfolds.

Both 2 Thessalonians and the Book of Revelation use the imagery of Mark 13:14. Both of these books contain overtones from Passion Week in their warnings about spiritual idolatry and apostasy. The Man of Sin, as with Judas the betrayer, is a "son of perdition," according to 2 Thessalonians chapter 2. "Perdition" is a synonym for "desolation." As for the Apocalypse (the Book of Revelation), its key resides in Passion Week itself, and especially in this final discourse of Christ's ministry. The corporate Christ ("the body of Christ," 1 Cor. 12:12) is represented in Revelation as paralleling the experience of its Head. All the characteristics of the Olivet discourse are reproduced in Revelation, including the peril from the abomination of desolation. See chapters 13 and 17 especially.

Apart from the primary exegetical issues, we have in this mystical phrase concrete imagery enshrining reminiscences of human depravity—that depravity which exists even within the hearts of worshippers of the true God. "Prone to wander, prone to leave the God I love," is the refrain concerning human nature, which sounds and resounds from the pages of collective and personal history. It has been said of Luther that he found that "the same tension (Romans 7:14 and Galatians 5:17) ran clean through the official Church from top to bottom. The inner conflict of his soul had a counterpart within the Church on earth" (Torrance).

This understanding of the permanent practical meaning of Mark 13:14 for all ages is not meant to deny the primary application of the verse to A.D. 70, or its ultimate application to Antichrist at the end of the age. Rather we are saying that true exegesis will recognize that this warning, like grace itself, "is relevant to all stages of life's way" (Kierkegaard).

The very form of this enigma, its complexities and haze, support the idea that "all true theology is intensely practical." All exegetes should remember that, "in biblical interpretation, the point at which we are pulled up with a halt, the point where we really reflect upon the meaning, and finally understand what is intended, is the point where we are offended" (Torrance). Will Herberg has reminded us that our religion, however sincere and well meant, is ultimately vitiated by a strong and pervasive idolatrous element (*Protestant, Catholic, Jew,* pp. 284-285).

What we are here asserting is Christ's recognition of the reality of evil, which is an abomination in God's sight. This reality will bring a final test to all men one day, and it carries tremendous overtones for belief and practice now. <u>Some things are evil, and we ought not to participate in them, or countenance them</u>.

The little word "ought" reflects our misery and our mercy, our grandeur and our despair. Ought one ever to use the word "ought"? Can anybody live without using it? Wherein lie the strength and the validity of this demanding term? Does anyone truly have the right to say, "you ought," or "you ought not"? There are three "oughts" in that sentence actually, for to talk of the "right" implies an "ought." An "abomination" in the Old Testament was any form of idolatry violating the first table of the Decalog, and "desolation" intimates murderous force, which violates the second table.

Can we not see that there is enshrined in the simple words of Christ a whole ideology, a practical, inevitable philosophy for all who claim to be sane? He is assuming the universe is moral, and that the moral laws have a moral Lawgiver to whom we are each responsible. To be the least sympathetic with the abomination of desolation is to incline towards evil and participate in guilt, for an abomination in its original sense meant idolatry—the preference of anything or anyone over the true God.

If we mean it when we say, "I ought," we signify that we ought, though the heavens fall. Elton Trueblood pointed out in his *Philosophy of Religion* that, "the deepest source of interest in literature, the most moving scene, which the world has to show [is] that of genuine moral struggle. Thousands of pieces of great literature, with their uncounted millions of readers, bear witness to this fact (p. 110)."

Ultimately all our decisions depend upon our *weltanschauung*—our philosophy regarding the world, its origin, and its meaning. What men will do when confronted by the abomination of desolation will depend on whether they take God seriously. Are they in the habit of being moral, or do they live at a venture?

Our moral ideals are not merely subjective, a matter of whims. If they were, we could never condemn any actions as wrong. But there is a significant agreement about right and wrong, which cannot be attributed to mere coincidence. This remains true though there are more people suffering from moral blindness than physical blindness. "Moral experience is an absurdity and a delusion unless there is a Divine Mind to whom our moral obligation refers and to whom we are disloyal when we fail" (Trueblood, p. 117). If moral values and duties are a reality, so must be the divine Lawgiver to whom all are responsible.

The same author has summed up the whole matter thus:

1. Moral experience is a true revelation of the nature of reality.
2. Moral experience is meaningless unless there is an objective moral order.
3. The objective moral order is meaningless unless there is a Divine Being.
(*Ibid.*, p. 114)

These truths Christ always takes for granted, and it is only because our civilization is very anaemic and very sick that we question them. The day is coming when we must show our hand. Will we obey the abomination of desolation, the final Antichrist, or shall we obey the One who loved us and gave himself for us?

Chapter Four

An Exposition of Mark 13:14 and Matthew 24:15

In some respects these are the most important verses of the New Testament. Christ here urges upon us a duty which could save a multitude of lives. Let us commence our investigation by considering the contextual setting of Mark 13—both literary and chronological.

Of great significance is the fact that the theme of Mark 13 and Matthew 24—judgment—coincides with the pattern of the preceding events in Passion Week. Christ's pronouncements of divine visitation upon Jerusalem, the cleansing of the Temple, the cursing of the fig-tree, the utterance of judgment parables (vineyard and rejected stone), the marriage of the King's Son, the woes on the Pharisees; all take place as a series of thunder claps of judgment. It is obvious that the prediction regarding the destruction of the temple is perfectly coherent with the preceding accounts of words and deeds that week. Judgment as foretold by words and actions is now crystalized into an extended discourse on the same topic.

But we must also relate the Olivet Sermon to the chapters which follow it. If we take Mark alone, we find that the key words of his thirteenth chapter occur repeatedly in his closing chapters. "Betray," "watch," and "hour" are key words of the sermon. The first of these occurs three times in Mark 13 and 10 times in chapters 14 and 15. "Watch" is found several times in Mark 13, and 14:34,37 should be compared with these references. "Hour" appears in Mark 13:32 and should be compared with 14:35,41.

In this way the Olivet sermon acts as a transition to the narrative of the Passion. It reveals who it is that is soon to suffer (his greatness) and is also predictive of the future of the church. In Gethsemane, three of the same four disciples mentioned in Mark 13:3 are given the command to "watch."

That word, occurring in both chapters 13 and 14, indicates that the Passion began the troubles predicted in chapter 13, so placing the apostles in Christ's succession on the path to glory via sorrow and crucifixion.

Not only are Mark 13 and Matthew 24 linked to the preceding and following chapters by the themes of judgment and suffering, but their temple allusions also place them in literary and logical connection with these chapters. For example, each of the five chapters of Mark covering Passion Week, refer to the Temple. See 11:11,15-17; 12:10,33,41-44; 13:1-4,14; 14:58 and 15:38. Mark, writing in the last decade before Jerusalem's fall, was familiar with the concept of the church as the new Temple. Even in *Qumran* the idea of the community being the Temple was well known. Paul gave expression to the concept repeatedly in his Epistles, which had circulated widely before Mark's Gospel. And in Acts 15:14-19 the fallen booth of David's house is said to be raised up by the influx of Gentiles into the church. In this way the forsaken temple of Israel found its fulfilment in the Christian church as the new Temple.

Mark 13 and Matthew 24 warn that the attack to be made shortly on the Temple at Jerusalem would be followed by a continuing tribulation for the church-temple, one that would not cease until he came who is the true Tabernacle himself. The promise of the Advent of Christ as the returning Shekinah links the themes of the chapters preceding and following the Olivet discourse. Judgment is two-sided, and brings not only punishment of the impenitent, but vindication to members of the suffering remnant who are loyal to the law of Yahweh.

The key verses of the Olivet sermon, warning of the last sign before the return of Christ, occur in a passage that is climactic in both its literary and historical contexts. We have already referred to that. Even the pictured geographical setting—the view of the rejected temple and city from the opposite hill— is pertinent to the significance of the discourse. The latter is presented as flowing naturally from the immediately preceding events. After the disciples have heard Christ's woes and his prediction that the temple would be left desolate, and its hypocritical worshippers be denied a view of him until they acknowledged the returning Messiah—it is then that the fate of the Temple is further discussed.

Verse 14 of Mark 13 not only occurs in a passage that is climactic, it is itself a crescendo. The same "when" that occurs in verses seven and eleven is associated with prohibitions. But here in verse 14 we have a positive instruction—"Flee!"

Similarly, to <u>see</u> is more than to <u>hear</u>. Lastly, "then" occurs in verse 14 alone. It signifies the time for long-awaited action. These facts indicate that verse 14 is indeed the answer to the specific request of the disciples for a sign of the coming destruction of the Temple and the end of the age. It is clear that the mysterious "abomination of desolation" must be something very specific, for it constitutes a signal of no mean importance. Thousands await it. Upon its recognition depend the lives of multitudes. The words of C. C. Torrey are worthy of note:

> The sign, unlike all the others, was one to be acted upon immediately. On what impulse do companies of men "flee to the mountains" in wild haste, leaving even their outer garments behind? Not because of some obscure, mystifying phrase, nor because of any happening which may or may not be portentous.

Documents of the Primitive Church, p. 30

In harmony with this is the presence of the article "the" with "abomination" in contrast to the anarthrous state of the signs in verses 7 and 8 of Mark 13. Whatever the "abomination of desolation" is, its significance must be apparent to those who anticipate its coming. It is no mere abstraction, or idealistic portrayal. It is concrete, menacing, stirring. Time is of the essence, for nothing is to be taken from the houses. Lives are endangered. It is no longer safe to stay in the city or to seek it as a place of refuge. "Seek rather the shelter of the hill country," is Christ's admonition. Remember that all the events before the destruction of the city and Temple in A.D. 70 have a worldwide application at the end of history.

Add to all of this the presence of the word "but." It must be given its full force. A note of contrast is thereby sounded. Christ has admonished the disciples that neither false christs, nor wars and rumours of wars—not even persecutions are the main sign to be awaited. In effect he now says, "but here now is the real thing, the crucial event"—the abomination of desolation!

But it is appropriate that we should begin at the beginning with lexicographical data. What is the meaning of the word "abomination," and second, what is the meaning in this phrase of the well-known term "desolation"?

Any concordance with Hebrew and Greek lexicons can help us here. In essence, the first word has to do with idolatry, and the second with devastation. Put together, an idolatrous power that has a ruinous impact is intended. It is of great importance to note that there are several Old Testament chapters that also link these concepts, using either these very words or their synonyms. See Jeremiah 4, 7, and 44 and Ezekiel 5-7. There are numerous examples of divine threats of desolation as a result of Israel's abominations.

A review of the significant Old Testament passages mentioned above indicates certain matters of significance for the consideration of our key verses. First, the abominations, as might be expected, are linked with idolatry and profanation of the sanctuary. Second, because Israel herself has thus violated the sanctuary, it is declared that God will permit others to come and profane the holy place (Ezekiel 7:20-23, etc.). Their abominations will bring the abominations of the Gentiles. Because they have repelled the presence of God by their idolatry and spiritual harlotry, the once Holy Land will become forsaken and desolate, by man as well as by God. And lastly, the intention of God's judgments is reformatory. "Then you will know that I am the Lord." "They will be loathsome in their own sight for the evils which they have committed."

The judgments are meant to bring Israel to her senses. In Mark 13 and Matthew 24 all these factors apply, except that the abominations of Israel causing the divine judgments are no longer those of outward idolatry, and there is no anticipation of national repentance. Once more the sanctuary is considered as defiled because of the lack of sanctity among the people, and they will see the abominations of the invading Gentiles as a result of their own abominations. The land and sanctuary will be destroyed because they have already desolated [deprived] them of the divine presence.

Idolatry was always the bête noire of Israel. It was the cause of most of her troubles, including her exile and captivities. Idolatry was a blasphemous repudiation of the Decalogue from Sinai—the words spoken and written by God Himself. The accompanying term, when linked with the first, likewise contravenes the spirit of the sacred law, for it involves harm done to living persons.

Here we are reminded that "law' is a central concept in the Book of Daniel. In the first chapter Daniel and his friends will not eat as others ate, because such food was probably offered to idols and may have violated the food laws of the Pentateuch. The image symbolism of chapters two and three again are warning signs in view of the second commandment. In chapter four the king exalts himself and thereby violates the first of the Ten Commandments, which demand a worshipful spirit and legitimate approach to the Creator of all. In chapter five Belshazzar is guilty of blasphemy, violating the third law of the Decalogue.

Chapter six violates the spirit of the first four commandments by demanding a type of worship contrary to that of Yahweh. Daniel is criticized and hated because of his loyalty "to the law of his God." In chapter seven the figure for Antichrist "thinks to change times and laws," or "the sacred seasons and the law," as one translator has it. In chapter eight the temple where the law ("the truth") was deposited is cast down, and idolatrous worship replaces the worship ordained by the sacred law. In chapter nine the three OT terms for human evil—"transgression," "sin," and "iniquity"—are dealt with and replaced by everlasting righteousness. The final section, chapters 10 to 12, repeatedly refers to the idolatrous persecutor of God's people who plays fast and loose with the sacred laws of God and the correct form of worship.

The law from Sinai demands righteousness, and this is a key word of the book. See Daniel 9:24 and 12:3, 4:27; and 9:7,16,18. It is an eschatological term, and in Daniel 9:24 it points forward not only to the Atonement on Calvary, but to the new earth. The key verse of Daniel 8:14 is the only verse embodying the keyword of vindication (or justification), and both in the Hebrew and Greek languages these words are about righteousness. The well-known term "justification by faith" can equally well be translated "righteousness by faith," and it is significant that commentator Heaton, when attending to Daniel 8:14, tells us that Paul adopted this term (justification or righteousness) in his teaching.[2] Daniel 8:14 in its wider meaning signifies that, at the end of time, God's holiness and all associated with it will be vindicated by the coming of an everlasting righteousness. Daniel 9:24 explains 8:14, and there the terms for human evil are replaced by "everlasting righteousness."

All of which amounts to this: the abomination of desolation is Satan's substitute for the divine law and gospel and as such wreaks devastation. The passages in Daniel, Revelation, and the synoptic Gospels referring to this power are telling us that in the Last Days only those loyal to the law of God and who know the true gospel can avoid the last great temptation, which will entrap almost all of earth's inhabitants.

The chief difference between humans and all other living things is the awareness of the reality of right and wrong. Much of every day is spent deciding what is right to do and what wrong is to be avoided. Even if like

---

2   Eric Heaton, *Daniel*, 1967, p. 195.

Jehoiakim we burn the Scriptures, God would remain, conscience and duty would remain, along with the sense of right and wrong. There was very good reason for the first of the New Testament Epistles to deal with the question, "How can righteousness be obtained?" Similarly, the theological stress over millenniums (Christ's vicarious suffering for us in his sacrifice on Calvary, as the divine provision to save us from merited wrath) becomes preeminent in importance for all of us.

Christ's mysterious phrase occurs in Daniel 9:27; 11:31; 12:11 and a closely parallel instance in Daniel 8:13. That Christ had his eye particularly on Daniel 9:27 is certain because it is the only case in Daniel where the abomination of desolation is specifically linked with the destruction of the city. But he knew that the reference to Daniel 9:27 would automatically and appropriately create attention to the other passages and this too was within Christ's purpose.

Chapter Five

The Abomination of Desolation in 2 Thessalonians—How Most on the Planet Will Be Deceived

From the time of 1 Maccabees until the writing of Mark, the phrase "the abomination of desolation" is unknown to literature. But the concept associated with the term—that of an eschatological opponent of God modeled on the lines of Antiochus Epiphanes—was well known. It echoes throughout Jewish apocalyptic from the writing of Daniel onwards.

As regards the New Testament, the synoptic Gospels all speak of the sign of the end when the Holy City is imperiled, and the great tribulation launched. Two of the Gospels use this phrase, and the third refers to the armies of the invader. But prior to the writing of the Gospels, echoes of Christ's eschatological discourse are to be found in the two letters to the Thessalonian Christians, and among these echoes are some concerning the "abomination." It is in these, the earliest Epistles, that the first reference to the danielic picture of the Antichrist is found. Just as our key phrase is unknown to literature from the time that 1 Maccabees was written. Therefore the expression "the man of sin," when it appeared, was a unique term in literature.

What Mark 13 is to that Gospel, and the eschatological discourse to the Synoptics as a whole, so is 2 Thessalonians to the Pauline corpus. In each case we are confronted with an atypical emphasis, which is apparently esoteric. One writer has said that, "to give a full account of the interpretation of 2 Thessalonians 2:1-12 would be almost the same thing as to write a history of Christendom." As some plants are best known for their thorns, so this passage is renowned because of its difficulties. As the Slough of Despond in *Pilgrim's Progress* was noted for its swallowing up of whole cartloads of instructions without benefit, so this passage of Scripture appears to have engulfed a multitude of exegetical tomes without having been rendered entirely luminous. It has been described as "probably the most obscure and difficult passage in the whole of the Pauline correspondence." From the days of Augustine many commentators have evinced an extraordinary humility when confronted with the task of exegeting this famous chapter. At this point, one sees some truth in the couplet:

Commentators each dark passage shun,
And hold their farthing candle to the sun.

If 2 Thessalonians 2 is an acknowledged part of the biblical sun, it seems to be a part blighted with spots. Its puzzling incomplete allusions were sufficient, doubtless, for those to whom it was first written, but hardly so for subsequent readers. One can own to a sense of frustration when studying the chapter—a sensation which is heightened by a review of its commentators. As Dean Farrar rightly said regarding the whole body of opinion on this passage: "that vast limbo of exploded exegesis—the vastest and the dreariest that human imagination has conceived." As in the similar case of Mark 13:14, there is no consensus of interpretation. It is quite certain that if any single group of exegetes is correct in its position, then the majority (meaning all others) must be wrong. Contributory to the chaos of views is the face value of Paul's Antichrist. The thought of a supernaturally-endowed villain oozing celestial fireworks from the tips of his fingers and toes has had little attraction for either the nineteenth or twentieth century mind, or that of our own day.

The key words of this chapter are "apostasy," "the man of sin," "temple," and "the son of perdition." Any interpretation of 2 Thessalonians 2 worthy of respect must grapple with these and suggest some explanations that give congruence to the whole. But before we venture into these fields let us consider the literary context of the passage.

The very first words of this chapter show that the ensuing passage is the heart of the letter and embodies Paul's main purpose in writing. Paul alludes to the fact that some had been shaken and excited by the belief that the day of Christ had begun, and that soon they would behold the Lord himself. Then Paul proceeds to argue against such a misunderstanding by clarifying the eschatological picture. He does so by reference to what he has earlier taught his Thessalonian converts. But this is not accomplished by a mere summary allusion. Rather, it seems that the Apostle is glad to spell out again some features of the coming crisis, which he anticipated as the prelude to the fulfilment of "the blessed hope."

The following chapter begins with a "Finally, brethren," intimating that his main purpose in writing had been discharged. It is therefore clear that the opening words of chapters two and three of 2 Thessalonians clearly reveal Paul's eschatological discussion as the conceptual, as well as the literary, center of the Epistle.

Relationship Between 1 and 2 Thessalonians and the Eschatological Discourse

The similarities between the Thessalonian Epistles and the Olivet discourse have often occasioned remark. These similarities extend not only to parallel concepts but also to verbal expressions. H. A. A. Kennedy, commenting on this passage says, "It is no exaggeration to say that Matthew 24 is the most instructive commentary on the chapter before us." Another scholar, J. B. Orchard, expresses the same conviction and believes that the Epistles to the Thessalonians "are fairly bristling with verbal coincidences and reminiscences of the eschatological discourse."

Consider the following parallels:
2 Thessalonians 2:1,2 and Mark 13:27,7
2 Thessalonians 2:3 and Mark 13:5
2 Thessalonians 2:3,4 and Mark 13:14
2 Thessalonians 2:9 and Mark 13:22

The comparison between the Synoptic accounts and the Pauline chapter shows that the same Greek words are used in the same sense and in similar contexts. Furthermore, some of these are extremely rare expressions. Some believe that there is a literary dependence here proved, but it could be that the original source was oral not literary. Christ's words regarding the last things made a deep impression on his contemporaries and were often repeated. Paul speaks of his use of traditions in his missionary work. What he passed on to others, he claims to have himself received. See 1 Corinthians 15:3.

Relationship Between the Eschatological Discourse and the Man of Sin

The "abomination of desolation" appears in a discourse, which has as its theme the end of the age and the coming of Christ. It is associated with a time of lawlessness and apostasy, of false claims supported by miracles, and a time of special testing for the elect through supernatural manifestations just prior to the return of our Lord. It is to be manifested in "the holy place" where "it ought not to be." It constitutes a key sign of the impending end and comes as a judgment upon those who have rejected the gospel. Judged by its Old Testament counterpart, the abomination of desolation consists of a power that is proud, blasphemous, and outrageously ambitious, arrogating to itself the position of deity. It supremacy is short-lived, and its success is the signal for its doom. It "comes to its end" with time itself, as a prelude to the setting up of the kingdom of God.

Turning now to 2 Thessalonians 2, the man of sin appears in a passage devoted to a discussion of the end of the age and the coming of Christ. He is represented as being lawlessness incarnate, and he epitomizes apostasy. His manifestation takes place at the end of time, and is associated with false claims supported by signs and wonders. He takes his seat in the Temple of God. This culminating apostasy is the certain sign that the day of the Lord has dawned, and the man of sin like the abomination of desolation is a judgment upon those who have rejected the gospel. The man of sin displays himself as God, manifesting a proud, blasphemous attitude against all other objects of reverential regard. His supremacy is short-lived, for the coming of Christ and subsequent doom quickly follow his manifestation. The parallels are both obvious and striking as well as of key importance for exegetes.

These parallels are representative only and could be multiplied. If one works in reverse and begins with Mark 13, the following elements find their counterpart in 2 Thessalonians—the warning against deception (v. 5); the claim to divinity (v. 6); the warning against needless fear (v. 7); the abomination (v. 14); trial (v. 19); false prophets (v. 22); the advent (v. 26); and the gathering (v. 27).

Both the Olivet discourse and the Thessalonian Epistle draw heavily from Daniel for their presentations, and this helps to explain why the same things are represented of each power. It is beyond refutation that the abomination of desolation and the man of sin point to the same phenomenon. With this in mind, let us test that conclusion by an examination of the key terms used by Paul in this epistle.

The Apostasy

Paul does not set about to give any special explanation, but proceeds on the basis that all he continues to say is pertinent to his initial reference. In the verses that follow, the apostasy is not given any independent part. Rather, it is the characteristics and behaviour of the lawless one which occupy the picture. Therefore one should not attempt to distinguish the apostasy sharply from the revelation of the great rebel. The latter is mentioned in the same breath as the former. His being revealed parallels to some extent the fact that the apostasy comes.

The word itself always signifies religious revolt, so far as the Scriptures are concerned. This is true of both Testaments. The classical usage referring to political defection is absent from the Bible. However, the present reference is an excellent example of the principle that a word must be given significance according to its setting, and not only according to etymology, or common usage. The setting here is undoubtedly that of a culminating worldwide rebellion of mankind against God.

Paul is not thinking primarily of Jewish apostasy. That event had already happened and the Apostle prefers to speak of their misplaced zeal than to use the present term. He yet has hopes for many of his race. Neither does Paul proceed to reflect upon Christian apostasy, although such could be included in his view as a contributory or minor feature. At the time at which he wrote there was little indication of any large-scale Christian defection, and in these present letters he congratulates the Thessalonians on their fidelity. But what we do find in this passage is a description of the maturing of evil and its final blossoming so as to fill the world stage. Satan's climactic effort to defeat God by seducing the majority of the race by signs and wonders is dramatically sketched. The result is to be a separation into two groups, those perishing, and those being saved. Finally comes the reference to judgment—"all will be condemned who have not believed the truth but have delighted in wickedness" (verse 12).

Thus "the apostasy" in this context denotes a widespread violent defiance of divine authority. This rebellion is to be fostered by miraculous signs authenticating error, resulting in false worship and idolatry as the precedents of the persecution of those who do not conform.

A key factor in interpreting the apostasy is the description given of the lawless one. His characteristic is also the characteristic of the apostasy that he epitomizes—"iniquity," "lawlessness." While this includes transgression of the divine precepts, it is fundamentally rebellion against God. Its primary meaning is not the legal sense, but rather an active personal hostility more malicious than the mere transgression of a norm of behaviour. Furthermore, this term has cosmic scope as the classic Qumran text (1 *QS*, III, 21) shows. So the basic nature of the apostasy finds its key in the nature of the great rebel here described.

Another important key to interpreting this apostasy is the contrast afforded it in the context by "the mystery of lawlessness" which, according to Paul, was already working. Evil is then and there at work in its hidden form. This is not to say that it does not ever become flagrant, but rather that in general it is characterized by subtlety and underhand activity. However, that which at present is veiled is soon to be manifested openly. With the man of lawlessness will come a violent upsurge of unrighteousness. No longer will it be cloaked or restrained.

Most of what Paul has to say, or has already said in person to the Thessalonians, has its seed in some previous revelation. Mark 13 and Matthew 24 had forecast the time when lawlessness would be multiplied. This event would be associated with the working of false prophets. Neither did this picture have its origin with Christ. Daniel, and other pseudepigraphical writings testified to the same. According to Daniel, a king of bold countenance would arise at a time when "the transgressors" would have reached their full measure. Apocryphal writings, produced just before and just after the beginning of the Christian era, amplify Daniel's allusions to apostasy. *Ethiopic Enoch* pictures worldwide anarchy and distress as characterizing the time of the end. The earth is to be filled with blood, the heavenly orbs will be worshipped and the Creator abandoned. Sin, injustice, blasphemy, violence in all its forms, apostasy and transgression will abound. In 4 Esdras the picture is similar. The inhabitants of the earth are to be seized with a great panic, truth will be hidden and the earth deprived of faith. Then iniquity would increase above that hitherto known.

Long before the pseudepigraphical writings, however, the concept of a final rebellion is to be found in the prophets. Gog and his hosts (Eze. 38,39), even all nations, would make war on God by attacking his people Israel. Later New Testament statements point to the same belief. At Armageddon the nations of earth have their rendezvous with God. They are pictured as gathered to make war on the Warrior who rides forth from heaven. And even beyond this point, after the millennium, the same scene occurs with Satan in the vanguard leading God's rebel armies against the Holy City.

It is no wonder, then, that we find the article "the" with the Greek term for apostasy. The event of which Paul speaks is familiar to his readers, both because of his own instruction, and because Jews and Gentiles alike already possessed prophecies of just such a climax to history.

In summary, Paul, by his reference to a coming apostasy, points to the eschatological rebellion anticipated by the early Christians. It comprehends a worldwide revolt against God, his gospel, and his law. It marks the rejection of Christian preaching and the acceptance instead of another gospel, even "the lie" offered by the man of lawlessness. This embracing of a false gospel leads to false worship of a pseudo-god. Instead of the fruit of the Spirit, the authenticating signs of the new gospel will be miraculous wonders performed with "all power." The key terms of this passage such as "iniquity" (lawlessness), "revealed," "perdition," point to the nature, time, and issue of the rebellion. At its heart is the man of lawlessness who enshrines in himself the self-idolatry, blasphemy, and hostility of the apostasy. His deceptions bring mankind to the test, separating the sheep from the goats and paving the way for the Judgment. The rebellion will be short-lived, for the height of blasphemy brings the true Christ whose very presence suffices to annul all opposition and to destroy the pretender. This presentation by Paul finds further illustration in the last apocalypse where the final rebellion finds its most detailed, though symbolic, description.

The Man of Lawlessness

Paul now characterizes a well-known figure. Four times he uses the article "the" in four descriptive phrases. The man of lawlessness and the son of perdition are Semitic in character and are not used by Paul elsewhere. Two of his four expressions are equivalent ("the son of perdition" and "the lawless one") and they, as well as the other two, connote rebellion, anarchy, and ruin. As Satan himself is the original rebel and destroyer, so this final representative of his is an opposer or adversary, and is not only himself destined for destruction but lures the perishing to the same fate. As with Lucifer of old, this being also desires to "sit on the mount of assembly," making himself "like the Most High," but he will be brought down to the depths of the pit. His session in the temple of God is succeeded by his dissolution at Christ's coming. And so, in remarkably small compass, Paul has sketched one in the likeness of the Prince of evil.

The literary marvel is magnified as we recognize that there is also another likeness incorporated into the same portrait. This figure not only resembles *Diabolus*, but also Prince Emmanuel. *Diabolus* is a parody of Christ, with an unveiling, a parousia, a fixed appointed time, possessing power to work signs and wonders, and claiming worship. Either Paul anticipates John, or John copies Paul, but both depict the Antichrist as a counterfeit of the true Messiah. He will be a counterfeit Christ offering a counterfeit law and gospel.

This matter of parody, or counterfeit, is probably implicit in the initial term used by Paul. The phrase "the man of lawlessness" is a literary parallel to the expression "the man of God." The LXX uses this latter term over 60 times as a technical term designating a prophet. Therefore, what we have in 2 Thessalonians 2 is an allusion to one who copies God's Man, but who is in fact the very opposite.

Here we have our best clues relative to the time, nature, and work of this Antichrist. If he is a counterfeit of Christ, like him he must be a single individual or institution. If he is to be unveiled by a *parousia* in glory, and is then obliterated by the coming of the real Christ, his time of manifestation is limited to the last of the last days. In the setting of 2 Thessalonians 2, Antichrist is one to be manifested at the end of time. His *parousia* is a sign that the end has come. Therefore, an interpretation that applies this passage to an individual of past history, or to a succession of such as completely fulfilling this prophecy, misses the mark.

The key features of Paul's description of the great adversary are drawn from the book of Daniel. See Daniel 7:25; 8:25; and 11:36-37 for "the man of lawlessness"; Daniel 7:11,26; 8:25; and 11:45 for "the son of perdition"; Daniel 7:8,20,25; 8:4,10,11,23-25; and Daniel 11:36-39 for "who opposes and exalts himself"; Daniel 8:9-14; 9:26-27; and Daniel 11:31,45 for "he takes his seat in the temple of God." See also Isaiah 14:13-15; Ezekiel 28:2,8 and chapters 38-39, and Deuteronomy 13:1-3. The reason for Paul's use of the passages from Daniel is not difficult to find. His predecessors and contemporaries firmly believed that Antiochus Epiphanes, the adversary predicted in Daniel, was the type or symbol of a God-opposing figure yet to come. Christ himself had endorsed this concept (Matthew 24:15), and Paul claimed that his own views of the end were derived from "the word of the Lord." See 1 Thessalonians 4:15.

We have noticed also that the lawless one appears only at the end of time. Not only his parody of Christ indicates this, but the whole context of the passage. He is the center of the apostasy, and the time-location of this phenomenon automatically limits his own chronological possibilities. "The apostasy" implies the separation of the good and the wicked, the ultimate divergence of the two opposed lines of development. The fact that he is to be "revealed" could not but remind the first readers that the same term had just been used of the coming Advent of Christ.

Next we would enquire as to the particular nature of the "lawlessness" to be manifested by this being, and whether or not, as most commentators suggest, he is to be considered as a member of the human species. One striking impression received, as one reads Paul here, is that this godless character he is presenting is ascetic in nature. There are no hints of any sins of the flesh. His are the sins of the spirit. The lawless one is primarily a rebel against his Maker, rather than a criminal or profligate. His particular fault lies in his self-deification. In 2 Thessalonians 2 we seem to have arrived at the opposite pole to Genesis 3. There the desire to be as God was indulged lightly, but here that particular sin has burgeoned and flowered. It is all a reminder for us of what was later to be written in Revelation 12 about Satan who himself is the Antichrist *par exellence.*

Not the least puzzling of the verses in this chapter is verse 4 with its reference to Antichrist as taking his seat in the Temple of God, proclaiming himself to be God. This implies a formal claim to occupy the central seat in men's minds that belongs to God alone. What we have here is the arrogant assumption of divine honors. It will involve his legislating decrees which will be an attempt to "change the sacred seasons and the law" of Yahweh. See Daniel 7:25 (RSV). His own religion must be distinguished from that of the One against whom he rebels, and counterfeits of divine institutions are to be expected.

The Old Testament frequently uses "man" for spiritual beings. See Daniel chapters 8, 10, and 12. Here this rebel is spoken of as being "revealed," almost as though he already existed, but was not yet manifested. Far more significant is the concentration of power invested in this personage. He works with "all power." To Paul and his contemporaries, it would have appeared much more likely that Satan would manifest himself through spirit beings in various places as an angel of light, than that Antichrist would be merely a fellow human. See Revelation 16:14. We should note that this Antichrist is not a power that exalts itself against God by denying the supernatural. He is not related to present-day atheists, who, in terms of the global history of the world, are a comparatively recent phenomenon.

First century Christians who studied both the Gospels and Paul's writings would have concluded that the anticipatory phenomena associated with the fall of Jerusalem was to be shortly enacted on a vaster scale. The writer of the Apocalypse was one such Christian, who incorporated the distinguishing elements of the end, offered by Christ and Paul, and applied them on a global scale. A final period of tribulation and testing, great apostasy, supernatural signs and wonders, and an idolatrous Antichrist characterize New Testament eschatology from first to last.

The Temple of God

Does this signify Jerusalem's Temple, or a heavenly Temple, or the Christian church? The term used does not signify an entire temple complex, but rather an inner shrine. And the repeated article "the" points to a well-known temple. Paul's rather contemptuous reference to the existing Jerusalem in Galatians 4:25 and his neglect of that place elsewhere in his writings, argue for the case that Jerusalem's Temple is not his real concern here. Paul's normal use of the term is with reference to the Christian church.

The remainder of the sentence concerning the temple has been too often neglected though it interprets the word in question. The temple session is equivalent to Antichrist's proclamation of deity. The whole section is a poetical description of the usurpation of divine prerogatives generally. As C. J. Riggenbach has suggested:

> In colors of his own time Paul depicts an act which, as a symbol of permanent spiritual significance, is confined to no locality, and means to say: He places himself in God's room, and forces himself on mankind as a Divine ruler.
> (*Thessalonians*, p. 128)

The Restrainer

The KJV reads mysteriously when it speaks of "he who letteth will let until he be taken out of the way" (2 Thess. 2:7, KJV). The term "let" here is old English for "hinder." So now we must ask, "Who or what is meant by the hinderer (he who letteth)?" Those who read the commentaries believe that the hinderer has become more famous than Antichrist himself. Many are the propounded theories, and the most popular one is that the hinderer signifies the Roman Empire. But Paul is not in the habit of making political references. In another work I have discussed in detail the various views of the hinderer (see *The Abomination of Desolation in Biblical Eschatology*—a book found chiefly in seminary libraries). Here I offer a view, which alone seems to meet all that is required.

The chapter itself offers some characteristics of the entity we seek:

1. It is a present force. The word used is a present participle, thus the obstacle was already a barrier at the time Paul was writing.

2. It is a beneficent force. The hinderer, or restrainer, holds back the full burgeoning of the mystery of iniquity into the Antichrist. It is the removal or withdrawal of this beneficent power from the midst that enables Satan to lead his representative (or himself) to success.

3. Thus on the principle of opposites, it would seem that this power is itself in harmony with the government of God. It is a law-abiding and law-upholding force, in contrast to the lawless one.

4. This power has a divine time-mission. As Antichrist is to be revealed "in his time," so will the hinderer hinder till his time has been fulfilled.

5. It is a power that actively withdraws, rather than one that is passively acted upon. There is no hint that it is to meet with any fate similar to that of Antichrist. It is neither to be "consumed," nor "destroyed." It merely moves out of the midst.

6. This power spans the ages, from the beginning of time to the end. We would now emphasize a truth of great importance and much neglected. It is implied throughout this passage that the eschatological rebellion is Satan's crowning effort. It is his master plan. This ultimate rebellion—with its dramatic claim to deity by the lawless one masquerading as Lord of the divine Temple—has not been postponed willingly from age to age by the great Adversary. Rather he has been foiled by God's power, the hinderer, and it has been so from the beginning.

   There are no grounds for believing that Satan has just conceived the rebellion in Paul's time, and therefore there are no grounds for believing that the hindrance and hinderer belong only to Paul's yesterday. There is every reason for understanding the passage as teaching that for as long as there has been a satanic force active upon the inhabitants of this globe, just so long has Antichrist been restrained by God's opposing agency. We should therefore look for an entity whose existence at least measures with the existence of evil itself.

7. This power, of necessity, must be an extraordinarily great and mighty one, if it is able to withstand a supernaturally-endowed being. A feather could crush a mosquito, but if we dare to exterminate a Hiroshima something of greater proportions is invoked. What alone could withstand the one known as, "the prince of the power of the air," a wicked spirit from the heavenly places, who could send storm and tempest and destroy with no boundary other than the permitted will of God?

A coherent explanation of this mystery is found by a *gestalt* of all the key elements and requirements of the passage. Paul's presentation was almost certainly that of a complex entity, rather than that of one or two parts. We think the evidence indicates that he discussed a situation rather than merely a power or a person, but a situation with certain basic emphases. In harmony with positions taken elsewhere in the New Testament we submit that the Thessalonians were taught that civil law would restrain the natural rebellion of human depravity for as long as the Holy Spirit moved on men's hearts urging them to yield to the gospel. It is perfectly clear that the great apostasy surrounding the coming Antichrist would constitute a unique event in the history of mankind. And therefore at that time some factor or factors would be missing that had prevailed hitherto throughout the entire history of the world. Logically it is this factor, or factors, which constitute the hindrance to the threatening rebellion.

Paul was aware that the Old Testament presented occasions when the pleading of the divine Spirit ceased, and with that event the closing of probation for some, leading to experiences of unmitigated rebellion ending in hopelessness, despair, and perdition. When Yahweh pronounced, "Ephraim is joined to idols, let him alone," then the next event to be expected was that those who had sown to the wind would reap the whirlwind. See Proverbs 1:24-31; Romans 1:24,26,28; Jeremiah 7:16, 11:14, and 14:11.

Paul himself had undoubtedly preached, as he was later to write to the Romans, that God "gave up" those who remained stubbornly impenitent (Romans 1:24). They were given over to a reprobate mind. He understood the *Torah* as teaching that—not only at the time of the Flood, but on repeated occasions when the warnings of the prophets had been rejected—the people had been left alone to fall into incurable rebellion against God. Had not Jeremiah been told, "Pray not for this people" (Jer. 7:16)?

Paul was also aware that in his own day Christ had spoken of the sin against the Holy Spirit, which would leave the guilty defenceless against the assaults and temptations of Satan (Matthew 12:28-36). The same Christ who had pronounced doom upon the race which rejected him, also warned that Israel would find themselves the victim of seven devils worse than the devil of external idolatry, which they had successfully exorcized (Luke 11:23-36). And it had also been said by Christ that after the gospel had been preached in the power of the Spirit to all the world then would come a time of great iniquity, trial, and deceptive miracles (Mark 13:10-22 and Matthew 24:11-24).

Therefore it was as clear as day to Paul that the worst rebellion could not possibly take place until mankind as a whole had rejected the good news of grace. Meanwhile the Holy Spirit, working through all benign institutions of the race such as civil law, would restrain man's natural wickedness. Man could not fall to the lowest depths until the pleading Spirit ceased to move upon resisting hearts. It was this factor of the moving of the Spirit upon all men, (although with limited power until Pentecost), which alone had prevented the race from sinking into abysmal depravity from the very beginning.

Second Thessalonians 2:10-12 points to the ultimate flowering of righteousness and iniquity, the maturing of the two groups—those being saved and those who are perishing, reflecting the Mary and Judas of John 12. It is made plain that those who have refused to receive the love of the truth will partake in the apostasy. Those who reject the gospel consent to "the lie" of Antichrist. They are without the divine panoply of the Holy Spirit and as a result are deceived by devilish signs and wonders. Twice in these three verses it is asserted that it is the failure to accept the gospel ("the truth"), which renders the race ripe for the ultimate rebellion. This same emphasis is found in the preceding chapter. Rest is promised to those who believed Paul's testimony to the gospel, but vengeance is threatened against those who "do not obey the gospel of our Lord Jesus." And in his previous letter Paul spoke of wrath coming upon the Jews because of their rejection of that gospel which alone could save them and the Gentiles.

It is clear that there is a linguistic and contextual similarity between the abomination of desolation of Mark 13:14 and the Antichrist of 2 Thessalonians chapter 2. Both powers are an abomination to God; both powers are a threat to his people; both menace the Temple of God; both constitute the sign of the end; and both are displaced by the avenging Christ. In the LXX, "abomination" is sometimes the equivalent of "iniquity" or "lawlessness," and "desolation" the equivalent of "perdition."

The key to the puzzle lies in the fact that Mark 13:14 transcends a limited historical application to the destruction of Jerusalem. Two levels of meaning are here. This probably explains why in the original Greek the subject is neuter, but the later participle is masculine. The first has reference to the attack on the Holy City in A.D. 70, and the second to the attack on the Israel of God immediately prior to the end. The one could quickly have merged into the other had the early Christians met with greater success in their proclamation of the gospel to the Jews and the world. While the subject of this terrible phrase is neuter, the genitive masculine case hints of the ultimate Antichrist.

In one sense the Holy Spirit is the hinderer, because, only while He moves upon men by the gift of "common" grace, does law retain its influence. Therefore, at a lower level, the human law-enforcement officers, themselves made willing to maintain the law, become the hinderer. In another sense the preachers of the gospel are the personal restraining influence, and the gospel preached becomes itself the hindrance for so long as its task of witness is incomplete. We should also take into account Daniel 10:5,13,20, which teaches plainly that angels act as restraining powers among human governments. The angel tells Daniel that, after he departs (compare Daniel 10:20 with 2 Thessalonians 2:7 "taken out of the midst"), then will come Antiochus, the Old Testament Antichrist. So the Christian church has opportunity for its work of proclaiming the gospel for as long as angels, as the instruments of the Spirit, move upon the leaders of governments.

In Revelation 9 we read two versions of wickedness restrained and bound, and in Revelation 20 we read a final instance where the final fling of demons and men is described. Only when God permits the unlocking of the abyss does the greatest of Antichrists, recovered from his deadly wound, ascend to battle.

2 Thessalonians 2 is indeed a challenge, but it is worth all of our prayerful efforts to find the treasure hidden in its phrases.

Chapter Six

The Abomination of Desolation and the Apocalypse—the Destruction of Antichrist

If the abomination of desolation motif has its seed in the book of Daniel, its "blade" is found in the Olivet Discourse; its "ear" is in 2 Thessalonians 2, and the "full grain" is in the last book of Scripture. It is doubtful whether the theme of Antichrist would ever have assumed more than footnote attention, but for its prominence in the Apocalypse.

As T. D. Bernard pointed out in a notable work (*The Progress of Doctrine in the New Testament*), the threatening clouds grow thicker and darker as one reads the New Testament. The meridian glory of Pentecost and the full flush of early Christian expectation begin to gradually diminish with the attrition of passing years. Several of Paul's Epistles warn of approaching troubles. In 2 Peter the warning intensifies, while in John's Epistles and the missive of Jude it becomes still shriller. But in Revelation itself, we have not only clouds, but storm and tempest. At this juncture Antichrist comes into his own and he is greatly angered, because he knows that "his time is short."

Of course, Antichrist is a genus, a kind, as well as a specific figure. All who oppose by cruelty, or counterfeit by subtlety Christ and his church, come under this heading. Satan himself, in the eyes of first century Christians, was the supreme Antichrist, and so Revelation 12 paints him. Better known by the title is his chief henchman of the last days, one who will employ signs and wonders, proclaim himself as God, and precipitate a time of trouble such as never was—"the hour of trial," which will "try them that dwell upon the earth" (Rev. 3:10). The final Antichrist, as sketched in Revelation 13, is not just an individual, but a corporate structure, a persecuting government.

The Relationships between the Abomination of Desolation in the Olivet Discourse, the Man of Lawlessness in 2 Thessalonians, and Antichrist in Revelation

It should first be said that such relationships should be anticipated if for no other reason than that the final apocalypse appears to be an expansion of all prior apocalyptic found in Scripture. While the Olivet discourse is not apocalyptic in form, it certainly embodies and reflects throughout apocalyptic motifs of which the abomination of desolation is chief. And it is a truth that has impressed almost all commentators that the book of Revelation is a thoroughgoing development of Christ's sermon on "the Last Things." It is just as certain that the writer has in the view the forecast of Christ on the last Tuesday of his life, as that Christ in that address has the themes of Daniel in mind.

In Mark 13 and its parallels, the abomination of desolation is linked with attack upon the Holy City, precipitation of an unparalleled time of trouble, miraculous signs and wonders, counterfeit christs and false prophets, before the ultimate coming of the avenging and rescuing Christ. In Revelation, the same theme of attack upon the Holy City occurs and reoccurs. It is synonymous with persecution or "war" against the saints. This "war" is the great subject of the concluding chapter of the first half of the book, and of the entire second half. It is specifically referred to in chapters 11, 12, 13, 16, 17, 19 and also in other chapters that do not use the word. While some have discounted any special attention to Armageddon on the ground that it is only mentioned once, what we actually have in this mention is the climax to a war, which is repeatedly alluded to and which dominates the thinking of the writer.

As the original abomination of desolation was not only a desolating invader who wore out the saints, but also one who claimed worship for himself, so it is with the chief earthly manifestation of Antichrist in the book of Revelation. And furthermore, as in Daniel, Mark, Matthew, and Second Thessalonians, this apparition was the immediate prelude to the setting up of the kingdom of God in glory, so is the case also in the Apocalypse.

Preparatory to a closer look at the passages concerned, some of the more obvious parallels pertinent to our subject will be indicated.

Daniel 8:13 speaks about "the transgression of desolation," which tramples underfoot the sanctuary and the host.

Mark 13:14 warns about the "desolating sacrilege set up where it ought not to be."

Second Thessalonians 2:3,4 speaks of "the man of lawlessness," "taking his seat in the temple of God."

Revelation 11:2 predicts that "the nations" will "trample" over "the holy city."

Note again that in Revelation 11 the Temple and Holy City are in focus. Again the worshippers are threatened, even "trampled," as in the initial reference. And again it is invading Gentiles who are responsible for the aggression and profanation, as was the case with Antiochus Epiphanes. The climax of devastation is reached when the beast from the bottomless pit successfully makes war on the Two Witnesses. But the triumph is brief, for vindication of the saints follows, and with it the kingdom of God on earth. Here is the parallel to the concept adjoining the verse in Daniel quoted above. After many days the sanctuary and its true worshippers were to be vindicated. This is how closely the first chapter of Revelation concerning the Antichrist clings to the initial apocalyptic sketch in Daniel on the same topic.

The opening chapter of the second half of Revelation also embodies Daniel's imagery concerning the work of Antichrist. We read in chapter 12 of a monster with 7 heads and 10 horns raking the stars from the skies, making war in heaven, and on earth pouring out a devastating flood to drown the escaping saints. The battle rages for 1260 days. Then for the final war on the remnant, the monster stands on the sand of the sea summoning a fearful henchman who will initiate the last slaughter.

All of this takes its rise from the Old Testament description of the work of Antiochus. He, too, was pictured as sky raking, and dashing the holy ones to the ground. He, too, invaded the Holy Land like an overwhelming flood. He, too, was pictured as the representative of a monster with 10 horns. His period of persecution likewise was for "a time, times, and half a time," or 1260 days. This number, also set forth as forty-two months or three-and-a-half years, is a symbol of trial (three-and-a-half is a broken 7). All attempts to turn the 1260 years into days, as historicists do, are erroneous. For example, there never was such a period (538-1798 A.D.) of Antichrist's supremacy. See my book, *For the Sake of the Gospel.*

The thirteenth chapter of Revelation continues the expansion of the Danielic picture. The earthly twin of the heavenly dragon appears, having the same number of heads and horns and doing the same work for the same length of time. He blasphemes the sanctuary of God and desolates its worshippers. His representatives perform miraculous signs and wonders to persuade those on earth to adore his image, which can both breathe and speak. Then comes the great martyrdom of the nonconformists, an obvious parallel to the war upon, and the death of, the Two Witnesses in the first presentation by John of the Antichrist theme. Many features of this chapter enhance the counterfeit aspect of the adversary, which had been stressed by the Olivet Discourse and by 2 Thessalonians 2. The chief figure of Revelation 13 is a member of a trinity; he has been slaughtered, but revives to resurrection life; he calls forth authenticating signs; he has witnesses who, like Christ's witnesses, can call down fire from heaven and he demands worship. A new feature in this chapter is the reference to an image, which is to be the object of reverence. This is a very definite allusion to the abomination of desolation motif. Even the number 666 reflects imagery found in Daniel (see Daniel chapter 3).

Chapter 14 of Revelation contains a warning against submission to Antichrist and promises special blessing to those who are to be martyred. The entire book of Daniel had the same purpose as this chapter of the Apocalypse. It also, from the first chapter to the last, had a didactic and warning purpose. The evils of the Gentile oppressor were sketched in graphic pictures whose point was in every instance "beware of this idolatrous oppressor." And Daniel is the prototype of martyrologies. Daniel 11:32-35 is the basis for all later variations on the theme. Such admonitions as Revelation 13:10 and 14:12-13 are but reminders of Daniel 12:2-3,10-13.

Revelation 15 pictures the ultimate victory of those who had refused to worship Antichrist and his image. The destruction of the desolator is seen to issue from the heavenly temple of which the desecrated one on earth was but a faint shadow. One familiar with Daniel, reading this chapter, would be reminded of many references in the Old Testament book coinciding with this theme.

Daniel had spoken of a heavenly Watcher who marked the pride of Israel's oppressor, and he had sketched the Judgment, which weighed the impious adversary in the balances and found it wanting. Catastrophic upheavals had brought old Babylon to its end and there had been none to help it. Daniel 9:27 had promised a "decreed end" for the desolator, and this end was to be "poured out" when the divine indignation was accomplished. Similarly,

Revelation 15 promises the pouring out of God's wrath upon Antichrist, even the emptying of heaven's bowls of judgment plagues. So would the consummation foretold by Isaiah and enlarged upon by Daniel be fulfilled. The message of Daniel and Revelation 15 is the same—"It does not pay to submit to Antichrist. The desolator will himself shortly be desolated."

The following chapter in Revelation still centers about the work of Antichrist and the divine response. The seven plagues are divided, as is usual with the sevens of Revelation, into four and three. Most attention is given to the second group, which describes the final battle in the war between the true and false Christ. In ancient times Antiochus had compelled men to be branded with the ivy leaf, the mark of Bacchus, but the writer of Daniel had warned that all who submitted to receiving such would become subject to "shame and everlasting contempt." Revelation 16 pictures the divine wrath descending upon "the men who bore the mark of the beast and worshipped its image." The origin of the mark in the forehead or hand is found in Deuteronomy 6:8; 11:18; and Exodus 13:9. It has to do with remembering the divine law and its precepts.

Those who have persecuted others are now persecuted, and those who have shed blood must now drink it. But the central emphasis in this chapter is upon the gathering of the kings of the earth "for battle on the great day of God the Almighty." The powers of chapters 12 and 13, namely the dragon, the beast, and the false prophet, are the leaders of this opposition. In fact, Revelation 16:13-14 is descriptive of the same crisis mentioned in the last half of Revelation 13. War is made upon God by compelling his people to worship the beast and its image, or die. The same powers are in view, and the same signs and wonders. The following chapter enlarges the identical crisis by use of different imagery, but the war motif remains. Concerning the 10 horns of the beast it is written that they "will make war on the Lamb," apparently by antagonism to "those with him," who are "called and chosen and faithful."

The initial references to this "war," it should be kept in mind, are found in Daniel's descriptions of the attack by the Antichrist of his day. Commentators on Daniel 9:26 frequently point out that the war here mentioned is a springboard for later references to the final eschatological conflict.

Revelation 17 describes Antichrist from another viewpoint, when the one who has shed the blood of the saints is characterized as a harlot arrayed in purple and scarlet, bedecked with gold and jewels and pearls, and astride the now familiar beast with seven heads and ten horns. The name "Babylon the Great" is yet another allusion to the Old Testament saga of Antiochus Epiphanes. Nebuchadnezzar, who had boasted concerning the "great Babylon" which he had built, thereby exemplified the pride of Antichrist. His kingdom city built upon the Euphrates becomes the symbol of the new Babylon and her allies, for the harlot is not only located upon seven hills, but also upon "many waters." The writer of Daniel had depicted the fall of ancient Babylon, an event associated with the "drying up" of the river Euphrates, as foretold by Isaiah. Even so, hints Daniel, shall be the flood of persecution unleashed by Antiochus be "dried up." As Isaiah's writings, well-known and repeatedly quoted by Daniel (e.g., compare Daniel 9:27 with Isaiah 28:22 and 10:23), had predicted that Babylon would "come down and sit in the dust," with "no one to save her," so the later seer said of the eschatological adversary that he, upon attacking the glorious holy mountain "would come to his end, with none to help him." And so Revelation 17 continues the application of the abomination of desolation "spoken of by the prophet Daniel."

It is evident that Revelation 17 delineates the crisis, which calls forth the judgments of the preceding chapter. But it does more. It, along with the following chapter, describes those judgments by employing other symbols. The 10 horns desolating and burning the harlot and the holocaust of the city are just alternative expressions of the fate depicted in the chapter concerning the seven last plagues. And all this symbolism has its roots in passages from Isaiah and Daniel.

It should be specially noted that the terms "abomination," "desolation," and "desolate" are linked with the person and fate of Antichrist in this chapter. The power, which had forced the saints into the wilderness of a persecution experience, is now itself to endure the wilderness of persecution. The eighteenth chapter reiterates this terminology.

The coming of Christ is symbolized in Revelation 19, but its occurrence is seen as the climax to the battle of Armageddon. The powers of Antichrist, the beast and the false prophet of Revelation 13, lead the kings of the earth and their armies. But their ultimate destination is the lake of fire. This latter symbol is reminiscent of the fate assigned to Daniel's Antichrist, which "was given over to be burned with fire." The angel's call to the birds refers back to the similar call recorded in Ezekiel when the powers of Gog and Magog from the north fell upon the mountains of Israel. Daniel's description of the last attack upon "the holy mountain" by Antichrist is modelled upon the Ezekiel passage—as is the reference to "the north," etc. The overwhelming inundation of Daniel 11:40-44 is reminiscent of Ezekiel 38:14-16, and the fate of the king of the north in Daniel 11:45 is identical with the fate of Gog and Magog upon the mountains of Israel. The Johannine reference to Armageddon incorporates the imagery of the mountains mentioned in Ezekiel and Daniel. Revelation chapters 16, 17, 18, and 19 all enlarge upon the destruction of Israel's attacker "in the latter days," "the time of the end." The fate wished upon Daniel's Antichrist has become the destiny assigned to the eschatological Antichrist of John.

There is yet another reference to the abomination of desolation motif in the Apocalypse. It is a final, climactic allusion. The attack made before the millennium is repeated after the 1000 years. Or, if we choose to follow the amillennial view, the same attack is pictured anew. Revelation 20:7-10 describes the hordes of Gog and Magog as coming, not now from the north, but from the four quarters of the earth after their resurrection, and led by the supreme Antichrist, Satan himself. Again the Holy City is menaced as in Daniel 11:45. Once more the abomination of desolation stands, "where it ought not," on the borders of "the holy place." But once and for all "he shall come to his end with none to help him." He is "given over to be burned with fire." And from the ashes of a desolated earth the seer beholds arising "a new earth." Now the new covenant promise is consummated and God descends to tabernacle with men. The kingdom has come indeed, with all its glory. Shut out forever are all those who have worked abomination. The once desolated saints are now vindicated as they bear on their forehead, not the mark of Antichrist, but the name of Yahweh—that ancient priestly inscription of "holiness unto the Lord"—figure of the primeval image of the Creator borne by the original sinless parents of the race. Such is the symbolic vision of the seer of Patmos, embodying and transforming on a larger canvas all that his predecessors had intimated.

Revelation 11—The Two Witnesses and Antichrist

The eleventh chapter of Revelation is both a conclusion and an introduction. It concludes the first half of the book and introduces the second. Most of the key elements which are to characterize chapters 12-22 here find enunciation— the attack upon the church as it proclaims the gospel during the final crisis, the rising of Antichrist from a state of apparent death, the real safety and ultimate vindication of believers, and the ushering in of the eternal kingdom in glory accompanied by judgments upon those who reject the gospel.

To detach the chapter from its own introduction in chapter 10 is to fail in rightly interpreting it. There we read of an angel astride land and sea with a little scroll open, proclaiming that there is to be no more delay, and that the mystery of God is now to be fulfilled as predicted by the prophets. John takes the open scroll, and on eating finds it sweet to the palate but bitter upon digestion. Then he is told, "You must again prophesy about many peoples and nations and tongues and kings." At this point our present chapter begins as John is given a measuring rod and commanded to measure the temple of God, its altar, and its worshippers. He is instructed:

> Do not measure the court outside the temple; leave that out, for it is given over to the nations, and they will trample over the holy city for forty-two months. And I will grant my two witnesses power to prophesy for one thousand two hundred and sixty days, clothed in sackcloth.

It seems that the contents of the open scroll includes the matter set forth in the eleventh chapter. Therefore the bitterness indicates the suffering coming to those who proclaim the sweet tidings of the gospel. And this suffering is to be worldwide, for the message goes to "many people and nations and tongues and kings." Furthermore, it is suffering during the final crisis, for there is now to be no more delay, but the mystery of the kingdom is to be consummated. So we have in chapter 10 clues to the meaning of the following chapter.

The temple of God, the Holy City, the two witnesses, the two olive trees, and the lampstands all symbolize the witnessing church. They witness to the truths contained in the Law and the Prophets (alluded to by references from the experiences of Moses and Elijah in verses 6-7), and they, like Joshua and Zerubbabel of old, have priestly and royal prerogatives and duties. It would be impossible for "men from the people and tribes and tongues and nations to "gaze at their dead bodies," if these were two literal corpses in the literal street of literal Jerusalem. The worldwide church is signified.

The sources of this passage are basically the following:

1. Daniel's abomination of desolation passages, especially 7:25; 8:13; 9:26; 11:31-35 and chapter 12.

2. Ezekiel passages regarding eschatological events. See particularly chapters 37 and 40.

3. Zechariah chapters 4 and 12.

4. The Old Testament narratives regarding Elijah and Moses.

5. The records of Christ's ministry, which may indicate that He too prophesied for 1260 days rejected of men, and then was crucified prior to his vindication in resurrection and ascension. Even verse 10 seems to be an allusion to the Gospel record. See Luke 23:12.

So this chapter gives John's understanding of what the future holds for believers. Soon they are to enter upon the great tribulation, similar to that of the days of Antiochus Epiphanes. Those who refuse to conform will be slain by the beast from the abyss, just as those who refused to receive the mark of the ivy branch and conform to the false worship surrounding the image set up by Antiochus were martyred in the second century B.C. "But," says John in effect, "remember that you are kings and priests like Christ your Master. You will not be treated worse than he. You are to be partakers of Christ's sufferings as certainly as you are to partake of his glory. Your inmost life cannot be touched. God has measured you, secured you, sealed you. In the courtyard of earth where the Lord suffered, you may lose this earthly life, but the life hidden with Christ in God cannot be hurt. Ultimately you will be vindicated before all, while your oppressors must suffer judgment."

Verse eight is of great significance. Here John tells us plainly that he is using metaphor and symbol. He also makes it clear that the spirit of Jewry, which crucified Christ, is to be the spirit of the entire world in their opposition to the church. The court outside the Temple is probably a symbol of the Babylonian world. "Leave out" would be better translated "cast out." Elsewhere the word has the meaning of excommunication, i.e. casting out. The believer's life is indeed in the world, and there it must suffer from all who echo the unbelief of apostate Israel. Thus the court points to the same as "the great city, which is allegorically called Sodom and Egypt, where their Lord was crucified." The court was the place for sacrifice and thus aptly signifies the persecuting world.

Verse seven is similarly important. Here we find the article "the" linked with the beast, which is now mentioned for the first time. This is in harmony with John's frequent use of prolepsis (anticipating coming materials). The beast is Antichrist, as the later chapters make clear. Like the abomination of desolation in Daniel, the beast persecutes the saints because their worship is not of him. He is victorious for 1260 days, and during that time he treads down the worshippers in the sanctuary. So both Daniel's visions and the prophecy of Christ in Mark 13:14 and Luke 21:24 are referred to. The beast, because of its desolation of the true worship, is indeed an abomination to the seer who portrays him. Later he will foretell that the desolator is himself to be desolated.

The abyss is significant in pointing to the nether world of desolation as his origin and destiny. He is from the abyss in the sense that Christ by his victory on Calvary has inflicted a mortal wound upon Satan and his representatives. Hence they have no real right to attempt to coerce the people of God. This is spelled out more clearly in the twelfth chapter, but for the present we should notice that rising from the abyss is to be equated with a show of life manifested by persecution. This gives the clue to the real nature of the healing of the mortal wound referred to in chapters 13 and 17. The same theme reoccurs in the chapter on the millennium. Satan is wounded afresh at the Second Coming of Christ, and consigned to the grave for a thousand years. But after that, the wound is apparently healed, and as of old, Satan goes forth to make war on the saints.

Thus Revelation 11 sets forth in seed form all that is to be enlarged in the following chapters, and in doing so it indicates the manner in which these chapters are to be interpreted. And throughout the whole story the reader can ever hear ringing echoes from the days of Antiochus Epiphanes, the abomination of desolation in the first great apocalypse. Scholars have long rejected the once fashionable application of this chapter to the French Revolution.

Revelation 13

This can be called "the Antichrist chapter" of the book, for although later chapters make reference to the same power and the crisis initiated by it, none give so much detail to the climactic time of trouble as is here to be found. This is the highpoint of the final drama.

Again our interpretation is aided by taking into account the preceding chapter. There the Atonement of Christ had been graphically pictured as the expulsion of Satan from the heavenly courts. The defeated adversary has great wrath "because he knows that his time is short." He stands on the sands of the sea watching for his last representatives who will set on foot his final desperate effort to spite and spoil the people and plans of the Lamb his conqueror.

Then is described the well-known beast with its 10 horns and 7 heads. John is seeing the Antichrist foretold by the prophets. What is then happening in the Asian province of the Roman Empire is but the breaking of the waters. The real attack has yet to be launched, and when it comes, a demonic potentate will be its leader, one from the abyss of death. John believes that what is coming is the final death throes of the serpent whose swirling tail will launch the earth-dwellers to perdition, and many of the saints to rest.

Allusions to the abomination of desolation pattern are many. The story of Daniel chapter three is pertinent as well as the visions of that prophet. Once more we have the well-known period of trial, "forty-two months," the same as indicated in Revelation 11:2-3. Again we have reference to "war" upon the saints, as in Revelation 11:7.

What seems to be new is the symbol of the two-horned beast which hereafter is known as the false prophet. But even here the theme of Revelation 11 is being reiterated, for the two-horned beast is an obvious counterfeit of the two witnesses. He also calls down fire from heaven and works mighty signs. He also is the representative of another—indeed he is his publicity and propaganda officer. One cannot help being reminded of Christ's warning about, not only false Christs, but also false prophets. We have both brought to view in the present chapter. John sees false religious leaders on a worldwide scale, apostate to God and in league with the dragon (Satan, Revelation 12:9), being thus enabled to work wonders. He has in mind the eschatological fulfilment of Deuteronomy 13:1-3 and the story of the false prophet Balaam who has been alluded to earlier in this book. See Revelation 2:14. Church and state will yoke, as in Christ's day, when opposing religious parties united over their hatred of the popular Rabbi and linked with the State in order to destroy him. The coming union, the ultimate Antichrist, will be aided by miracles through the power of the dragon, and thus the majority of men will be enlisted to make war on the Lamb. This combination of the beast and the false prophet and their ensuing activities is discussed again in Revelation 19:17,19. No better commentary on chapter 13 can be found than in those verses.

Revelation 13 is thus the gathering for Armageddon—the final conflict in the controversy between good and evil, a conflict to be ended by the return of Christ. John is saying that the last conflict like the first (Cain and Abel) will be about worship, and will involve death. As in the original instance there will be a marking of separation. So severe will be the struggle that the majority of earth will join the devil and his associates. While a warning message from the witnessing church strives to save men from worshipping the beast and his image and endeavours to turn them to the worship of the Creator, the multitudes instead will become subject to the adversary of God and receive his mark, (the symbol of his character and his likeness).

The mystic number 666 has ever been associated with the serpent (a six combines both the snake and the sun, and the sun has long been associated with pagan worship). It is the number of sin and imperfection, attenuated to a trinity as if to indicate evil to the ultimate degree. It represents all that belongs to man when separated from God. It is truly "the number of man"—man under the serpent's control. And even here are overtones from the original abomination of desolation pattern, for in that source, too, the number six is repeated in connection with false worship. (See Daniel 3.)

Revelation 14 and 16

In chapter 14 is pictured the outcome of the last battle. The victors stand with Christ upon the heavenly Mount Zion. But having given that glimpse of triumph, the seer then proceeds to present the final warning to the world about its last fatal choice. It has to do with the "everlasting gospel." Revelation 14:6-12 pictures the fulfilment of Mark 13:10. It places earth-dwellers in a dilemma. They stand indeed between the devil and the deep crystal sea of God. While the beast threatens death to those who refuse to worship him, heaven thunders a pause to all who contemplate submission. The fall of Babylon, the oppressor, is foretold in order that men might not consider it invincible. The obedient are characterized as possessing endurance and the faith of Jesus, which is authenticated by their obedience to God's commandments. They are a "gospel" people. A special blessing is pronounced upon them. Then appears the sign of the Son of Man in heaven as he comes to redeem his own and destroy their persecutors. That sign is the counterpart of the abomination of desolation sign mentioned earlier.

The symbolism of the vintage harvest has been gleaned from the Old Testament pictures of divine indignation against the wicked. But let us enquire—"Why is the scene of destruction placed outside the city?" Here we have another illustration of the homogeneity of the biblical eschatological themes. The time of trouble such as never was is to be launched by the abomination of desolation (also called "the king of the north") surrounding the Holy City (Daniel 11:45). Then Michael comes to deliver his beleaguered saints. See Daniel 12:1-3. The view is similar to that of Joel chapter three and Ezekiel

38-39, which also picture the attack upon the city of the saints "in the latter days." John uses the same idea in Revelation 20:8, where the final employment of this symbolism occurs. In Revelation 14:20 John comforts the church with the assurance that in the last onslaught (Revelation 13), the saints will be eternally secure whatever their earthly fate.

John knew that Joel 2:32 promised deliverance from the foes gathered outside the city. Similarly Joel chapter three pictures a harvest in the valley of Jehoshaphat (Judgment), which lay outside Zion. It is this same harvest which John describes as the harvest of the earth. He also applies the treading down referred to in Joel 3:13. Those, who in days past have trodden down the Holy City, are themselves now trodden. But meanwhile the saints composing the city of God are eternally secure. The 1600 furlongs is the circuit of the "the holy oblation" of Ezekiel's vision, in which figured a mighty temple and city on the "very high mountain" in the land of Israel. The writer of the Apocalypse applies the "oblation" of Ezekiel to the worldwide church—outside of which the enemies of the church perish in Armageddon's slaughter. So, the treading of the winepress in Revelation 14, the bringing of the abomination of desolation to his end, the harvest in the valley of Jehoshaphat, the feast upon the slain of Gog and Magog, and the desolation accomplished at Armageddon, all point to the same event—judgment and destruction upon those who seek to destroy the people of God.

In the End, Calvary

In Revelation 16, the drying up of the river Euphrates, the kings of the east, the gathering of the kings of the whole world, and Armageddon are symbols which call for particular attention. The first two symbols are borrowed from Isaiah who foretold a drought upon Babylon's waters so that Cyrus might overthrow the city of Babylon (Isaiah 44:27; 41:2). Cyrus was God's Anointed—a type of Christ, a good shepherd, and the "one from the east." Such was the precursor of the deliverance of Israel from Babylon. The last Apocalyse asserts that, when the 10 horns turn upon the whore, "the peoples, and multitudes, and nations and tongues"—represented by the waters of Euphrates—cease to be her support.

It is important to understand that Scripture speaks chiefly of Christ and his church, and other powers only enter the picture when they have some relationship with the people of God. We must be careful not to interpret "the kings of the east" by the yellow journalism of the early part of the last century.

Anatole (east) was a familiar symbol for the Messiah in New Testament times. It pointed to something or Someone of heavenly origin. Elsewhere (Revelation 7:1), the Apocalypse uses the term in this manner, and it is hardly likely that a book so carefully written would change the meaning of this symbol in the later chapter. The "kings of the east" are intended as a direct contrast to "the kings of the whole world," mentioned in the same paragraph. They represent heavenly beings, who come to deliver the saints, just as the Median Kings from the east came with Cyrus to deliver Israel of old from Babylon. Ezekiel 41:2 pictures divine glory coming from the east, which was ever the route of entrance to the sanctuary. It is the return of Christ which is imaged here.

These symbols are of particular interest to the student of Scripture because the attacks of the abomination of desolation upon Israel are often represented as a "flood." Euphrates is used in Scripture as a symbol of an invading force. See Isaiah 6:6-8. In Revelation the Euphrates represents the multitudes supporting Babylon, and it is these multitudes, that are gathered by the dragon, the beast, and the false prophet, to make war on Christ by attacking his church. Euphrates and Babylon are part and parcel of Antichrist.

The "battle" mentioned in 16:14 is but another phase of the war referred to so often in the other chapters of this book. And the term Armageddon (often interpreted as meaning "mount of slaughter") conjoins the Old Testament memories associated with Megiddo with Ezekiel's prediction that the enemies of Israel will fall "upon the mountains." Daniel has Megiddo in mind when he speaks of the king of the north coming to his end "between the seas and the glorious holy mountain." The location fits Megiddo, across which plain invading armies poured when en route to attack Jerusalem. All these symbols in Revelation chapter 16 link the final battle with the crisis of Revelation chapter 13.

Revelation 17

In Revelation 17, Antichrist is pictured as the "mother of harlots and of earth's abominations." It is declared that ultimately she who has desolated others by martyrdom will herself be made "desolate and naked." Babylon as a symbol of false religion fittingly personifies in this chapter the whole world in religious apostasy from God. The name is, of course, reminiscent of Babel as well as of the kingdom of Nebuchadnezzar. The Tower of Babel in Genesis 11 shows how unconverted and vain man is—ever trying to climb to heaven by his own efforts as he discounts the clear commands of God.

Babylon, the whore, is an obvious contrast to the woman clothed with the sun mentioned in chapter 12. She is the consort of Satan—the very opposite of the church of Christ, encompassing all of all ages who have rebelled against the true worship of the Most High. The emphasis now is on the eschatological phase of counterfeit religion. In the last days one is either numbered with the woman clothed with the sun or with the harlot Babylon. Throughout the letters to the Seven Churches we have warnings intended to save Christ's flock from compromise. "The synagogue of Satan," "Balaam and Balak," and "Jezebel," are the early symbols of Babylon. John desires to save "half-baked" Christians from becoming Ahabs. All this must be kept in mind as we contemplate the picture in Revelation 17. It is succeeded by a call to separate from Babylon (18:1-4), and so indicates that more than geographical locations are in focus.

While it is true the Scripture used the harlot symbol for cities such as Tyre and Nineveh, it is much more frequently applied to the apostatizing people of God. See Jeremiah 2:33-34 and 3:1-11 where Judah is a harlot (2:20) with a sign upon her forehead (3:3), and "on whose skirts is found the lifeblood of the guiltless poor" (2:34). She is clothed in crimson (4:30) and golden ornaments. Her lovers will despise her and seek her life. We are reminded, too, that the same thing is written of Babylon as was addressed to faithless Jerusalem: "in her was found the blood of prophets and of saints, and of all who have been slain upon the earth." Compare Matthew 23:35.

The call to flee from Babylon should be linked with Christ's admonition to flee from the abomination of desolation. Only such withdrawal can save the soul. How appropriate the admonition, how artistically placed when we recall that Revelation 18 is the fifth consecutive chapter dealing with the destruction of the rebellious worldlings. In chapter 14 the theme began with the announcement, "Fallen, fallen is Babylon the great." The destruction by the treading of the winepress tells the same story. In the following chapter, a solemn pause accompanied the preparation for the outpouring of God's unmingled wrath upon Babylon. Chapter 16 describes Babylon's plagues. Chapter 17 show why Babylon deserves such punishment—it is because of her rebellion against God, her idolatry, her pride, and her persecution of the saints. Chapter 18 enlarges what was commenced in the preceding chapter, which foretold that the 10 horns would desolate the whore and burn her with fire. Such was the fate of a priest's daughter if she played the harlot, and such would be the fate of a fallen church to whom Christ came but who received him not. Her failure to recognize the divine Lover would be her undoing, and the burning of the city is only another metaphor for expressing the fate already suggested in the preceding chapter. Therefore, says John, "Flee!" And all who read it would be reminded of Christ's warning to flee from the guilty city of Jerusalem as Antichrist, the abomination of desolation drew near.

Also in chapter 17 we find a parallel to Revelation 13 and its description of the healing of the deadly wound. John says that the beast upon which the woman is borne has seven heads, and of these five are fallen and one is, and the other is not yet come. The beast finds its identity in each of the succeeding heads, the powers through the ages, which have persecuted Christ's people. Therefore it can be said to not be, though it once was, and that it shortly will be again. Even in this place, seven has the same symbolical meaning as elsewhere, and there are 53 other cases in this book.

Thus the five heads represent all who have gone before as Satan's representatives. The number six refers to the existing evil time about to give birth to the final Antichrist, the seventh head of the beast. The number eight is the symbol of resurrection and new beginning, to remind the readers that the beast would yet again ascend the abyss and demonstrate his revived life by a flood of persecution. The powers of earth united under the ultimate demonic Antichrist by the spirits of demons constitute the seventh head. There are not eight heads, only seven, but the seventh is called the eighth to show its parody of him who is the Resurrection and the Life, and whose number is 888.

Revelation 20

Most of the motifs of the preceding chapters recur once more for their final outworking. Again the beast rises from the abyss, again he assembles by deception the kings of the earth, and again the object of attack is the Holy City. But this time, the doom that falls upon the abomination of desolation is complete, and he receives his deserved recompense.

The great rebel who sought to make all men worship him, and who employed force to do so, "comes to his end, with none to help him." Simultaneously the objects of his attack become aware that the unending conflict has at last ended, and that temptation and trial will be no more. They luxuriate in the joy of their Lord, bearing his mark (his likeness) and bask in his glory throughout the ages. Such is John's story, John's painting, and John's undying music.

Hermeneutics

The word means merely principles of interpretation. Some readers will question what has been written in the preceding pages on the grounds that it seems to be based on a system of interpretation they reject—Futurism, or Historicism. But neither system is followed here.

The most popular form of Futurism is that adopted by the dispensationalist school, including such popular but unbiblical writers as Hal Lindsey. It is noted for bizarre, even fantastic, views of the future as the book *The Late Great Planet Earth* demonstrates. This form of Futurism holds that the future belongs to Israel after the flesh—not the church. More respectable Futurists insist that the book of Revelation is chiefly about the very last things and has had only a limited significance for earlier generations.

In this book neither Preterism or Futurism has governed the interpretation offered. And Historicism also is ignored. In these pages we have exegesis, the evoking of the meaning of the text without being governed by any system. This is the only acceptable approach in halls of learning, such as the great universities. It is the approach adopted by those scholars acknowledged as leaders in the field of exposition.

Most readers of this book have been exposed to Historicist interpretation since they first heard of prophecy. What failings does this system have? In 1989 a Seventh-day Adventist leader, Kai Arasola, wrote the book *The End of Historicism* for his doctoral dissertation. We recommend it highly. He documents meticulously the shortcomings of Historicism.

It is true to say that biblical scholarship today rejects Historicism because it violates the standard principles of interpretation and endeavours to accommodate prophecy to past or present events by illicit means. Historicism delights in finding important dates in the Bible, and particularly those concerning the Papacy. A representative of the SDA denomination had something to say on this at a court of law:

> Although it is true that there was a period in the life of the Seventh-day Adventist Church when the denomination took a distinctly anti-Roman Catholic viewpoint, and the term "hierarchy" was used in a pejorative sense to refer to the papal form of the church governance, that attitude on the church's part was nothing more than a manifestation of widespread anti-popery among conservative

Protestant denominations in the early part of this century, and the latter part of the last, which has now been consigned to the historical trash heap as far as the Seventh-day Adventist Church is concerned.

Sworn affidavit in the Merikay McLeod Lawsuit, page 4, footnote #2, docket entry # 84 EEOC vsPPPA, C-74-2025-CBR, February 6, 1976, at *http://en.allexperts.* Com/q/Seventy-Day Adventists-2318/hierarchy-Seventh-Day-Adventist.htm, (accessed 9 Oct, 2007)

Reinder Bruinsma, secretary of the Trans-European Division of SDAs suggested that "official Adventist prophetic interpretations have not made any dramatic changes in recent history." Then he adds:

As a result, Adventist understanding of the historical role of Roman Catholicism and of the end-time drama—with Catholicism as one of the key players—has remained basically unaltered. … The traditional arguments or the anti-Christian nature of Roman Catholicism continue to be heard. … more carefully worded at present than in the past. … The Seventh-day Adventist church faces a problem. What does it do with end-time prophecies that are rooted in a nineteenth-century interpretation of the world?

"Adventists and Catholics: Prophetic Preview or Prejudice?" *Spectrum*, Vol. 27, Summer, 1999, pp. 45-52

More important is the plain statement by Christ that forbids us to seek to know precise dates from the prophetic word. See Acts 1:7. Much more on this topic is to be found in my commentary on Revelation, *Crisis!*, Volume 1 and in the more recent work *For the Sake of the Gospel.* See also *The Adventist Crisis of Spiritual Identity.* We will content ourselves at this point with two illustrations.

In Revelation 13:3 we read that the Antichrist beast was wounded to death, but later came a healing of that wound. Adventists have applied this prophecy to 1798, when General Berthier took the Pope captive. But the wording of Revelation 13:3 springs from well-known symbolism originating first in Genesis 3:15, but amplified by Romans 16:20, Hebrews 2:14, Colossians 2:14, and Revelation 12:7-10. The "wound unto death" is what Calvary inflicted upon Satan, and it has nothing to do with eighteenth century history. The word translated "wound" in Revelation 13:3 is elsewhere translated "plague," signifying divine punishment.

Historicism has limited the term "antichrist" to the Papacy. But John tells us in his first Epistle that there are many antichrists. See l John 2:18. Ellen White was more accurate than her contemporaries when she wrote, "Antichrist, meaning all who exalt themselves against the will and work of God" (*Selected Messages,* Vol. 3, pp. 402).

The standard guidelines for exegesis are Chamberlain's Rules:

1. **Lexical**—This involves the specific meaning of each word at the time when it was used and harmony with the Bible writers' customary usage.

2. **Syntactic**—To interpret syntactically means to interpret according to the grammatical principles known to exist at the time of writing. The tenses, the use of the article, the dative case, etc., must be taken into account in the study of the LXX or Greek New Testament; the states of verbs, the significance of the inseparable prepositions and pronominal suffixes, construct state, etc., in the Hebrew Old Testament.

3. **Contextual**—The interpreter takes into account what is written prior to and subsequent to the very passage he is studying. He must inquire regarding the trend of thought to be found in the whole document, as this casts light on every part of that document.

4. **Historical**—Inquiry is made as to the circumstance that called forth this particular writing. Also the manners, customs, and psychology of the people among whom the document was produced will be considered.

5. **According to the Analogy of Scripture**—This principle recognizes the divine unity running through the Scriptures. All the passages bearing upon the one subject are gathered and compared, in order to find the teaching of the whole Scriptures on that given subject. This particular rule is especially important in the interpretation of Daniel because (1) its prophecies consist of a series of visions, which run parallel to each other, and (2) the entire eschatology of the New Testament interlocks with and casts light upon this Old Testament apocalypse.

In this connection it should be stressed that grammatico-historical exegesis, while giving primary attention to the literal meaning of the words of the passage, does not deny the presence of figurative, poetic, and symbolic elements. For example, most of the prophetic books are written in poetry. The apocalyptic writers are usually the exception to this rule, using prose for the most part.

We trust that this explanation will be helpful to some readers. See the books mentioned above for further information.

The Gospel to All the World?

While Scripture is emphatic that despite what seems almost a universal current of unbelief, in the last days the true Gospel will be sounded to every nation, tongue, and people. Naturally for many this sounds like an exorbitant claim. How could it possibly be fulfilled? Atheism is growing in the western world and only in countries like Africa, South America, and China is there obvious progress for the Christian faith. Can this ever be altered? Are the prophecies to be taken seriously?

A parallel case will now be offered where a similarly impossible project has been fulfilled already.

One of the most astounding passages in the Old Testament is the promise made to Abraham that his name would become great, that he would be a blessing to all families of the earth. See Genesis 12:3. That's amazing! Here was a nomadic sheik unknown to almost all the inhabitants of earth, a man without wealth, power, or influence, and yet one day he would be universally known and praised. But it has happened. Today the Muslim world, the Jews, and two billion Christians trace their spiritual ancestry to this ancient wanderer.

One of the most significant things about the Bible is its presentation of Israel's hope over millenniums, that one day her faith would ultimately be accepted by representatives of all nations on earth.

R. W. Church preached on this topic over a hundred years ago and among many other things he said concerning tiny Israel:

All around was darkness, with them was this little speck of light. All round were "gods many and lords many"—gods of the mountains and the valleys, of the heavens and of the earth, of the living and the dead, worshipped and trusted in by each nation, or tribe, or household. Out of them all, they had been selected to know the name of the One Almighty and Eternal. They, they alone, knew the truth about the world, its origin, its government. ... But from the first they were taught, that they knew this in order that the world might know it. ... How it was to be—how the knowledge and the blessing with which they were charged was to be passed over from them to the multitudes of the heathen—how the Gentiles were to be fellow-heirs with them—this was not told them. ... This is one of the things which make the religious history of the Bible unique in all that we know in this world.

Yet, with all its narrow exclusiveness, with all its insignificance, with all its isolation, amidst an uncongenial world, stationary when others were advancing, lost in its little corner while others were dazzling mankind with their glory and their might—Israel obstinately maintained the same conviction that its faith and worship were to be the faith and worship of mankind. ... Is there not something perfectly overwhelming to mere human judgment in the audacity with which Psalmist and Prophet—the Psalmists and Prophets of an obscure race, cut off by barriers physical and moral from the great scenes of human history—dare to claim for their faith, for their God, what no one else dared to do—the inheritance of all the nations, the spiritual future of all mankind? ...

The promise still remains, handed on by the elder to the younger Church. They built their hopes upon it, and now we build ours. But it comes to us with the illumination of something yet more wonderful than even itself. To us it comes interpreted by events which have for ever changed the whole aspect of the world, and history, and human life. ... What the promise meant is told us now in the songs of Christmas, and the Lenten memories of temptation, and the dumb awestruck contemplations on Good Friday of the Agony and the Passion, and the triumphs of Easter and Ascension Day, and the new world and the new creation of Pentecost.

Pascal, pp. 145-150

Despite the unbelief of our times it remains true that the spread of what was once the faith of an unknown tribe is the most significant event of all history. And no one would ever have predicted it—except inspired prophets. And now we await the fulfilment of a similar phenomenon—the Christian gospel offered to all on the fringe of eternity. Be assured that it too will be fulfilled.

Chapter Seven

Old Testament Previews of the End

Scripture says, "that which is to be hath already been" (Ecclesiastes 3:15). See also l Corinthians 10:11. As Leviticus contains types of Calvary and Christ's priesthood, so the historical books contain previews of eschatological events. Here are some of them:

Cain and Abel (Genesis 4)

Here is the first worship event, the first death, the first murder, the first marking, and the first judgment after Eden. It is also the first fulfilment of Genesis 3:15. The final war of the world will be over worship. It is called Armageddon, but it is described in several places in Revelation. See our earlier comments on the Apocalypse. Cain represents him who was "a murderer from the beginning" (John 8:44). According to Revelation 13, Antichrist will threaten to murder all who do not receive his mark and worship him. But, as in Genesis 4, God is not asleep.

It is highly significant that the first conflict was over religion, for the first anticipates the last, and Scripture has scores of illustrations of that relationship. When mankind has tried science, education, economics, politics etc to bring order out of chaos it will finally resort to religion—a religion of the lowest common denominator. Such a religion in all ages has had to be supported by brute force. So it will be in the eschatological future.

The Flood (Genesis 6-9)

The Flood story has tremendous symbolic significance. In chapter 6 we read what the world was like before it ended. Violence filled the earth and men took wives of all which they chose. In other words, the law of God had been made completely void. What a picture of our own day when the world is filled with violence and all forms of immorality!

Picture what would have happened in a world obviously near its catastrophic end with only a few in a safe place! Masses of violent men would have hammered at the door of the Ark wishing to get in, as volcanic eruptions threatened to engulf them. It would have seemed that the tiny saved elect were in danger of violent death. So will it be at the end of time. While many saints will be martyred, God plans to shelter a remnant to greet the returning Saviour.

Jacob and Esau at *Mahanaim* and *Jabbok* (Genesis 32)

Jacob nearing home wrestles with God at the *Jabbok,* fearful that his past sins might prevent God protecting him from what he interpreted as the murderous designs of Esau. This is the first instance of what later was called Jacob's trouble. It typifies the experience of the people of God in the very last days when fear of a murderous world leads to much heart-searching, prayer and agony. It also typified Christ's wrestling in Gethsemane on the edge of Calvary as the world's guilt was placed upon him. God's people too, the body of Christ, will repeat the experience of their head. Gethsemane and Calvary await us. But so do the glorious Resurrection and Ascension.

Jacob became Israel—the Overcomer—by holding on to the heavenly Wrestler despite his guilt and his fears. The last generation of saints will not feel that they have anything to boast about. Comparing their character with that of the Redeemer, it will seem that they deserve only destruction, yet by faith they cling to the loving Saviour. Jacob represents every believer. We have all been supplanters, placing ourselves above the will of God. But the mercy of God is infinite for all who take hold of him by faith.

Israel at the Red Sea Facing Destruction from Pharaoh's Host (Exodus 14)

In the last crisis of the church it will seem that ahead lies nothing but barriers, and behind will be a surging mob of idolatrous murderers. Sight offers no relief, but by faith it will be like when "the people passed through the Red Sea as on dry ground; but when the Egyptians tried to do so, they were drowned" (Hebrews 11:29).

One devotional writer has drawn the relevant lesson for all of us:

> Often the Christian life is beset by dangers and duty seems hard to perform. The imagination pictures impending ruin before and bondage or death behind. Yet the voice of God speaks clearly, "Go forward." We should obey this command, even though our eyes cannot penetrate the darkness, and we feel the cold waves about our feet. The obstacles that hinder our progress will never disappear before a halting, doubting spirit. Those who defer obedience till every shadow of uncertainty disappears, and there remains no risk of failure or defeat, will never obey at all. Unbelief whispers, "Let us wait till the obstacles are removed, and we can see our way clearly"; but faith courageously urges us to advance, hoping all things, believing all things.
>
> The cloud that was a wall of darkness to the Egyptians was to the Hebrews a great flood of light, illuminating the whole camp, and shedding brightness upon the path before them. So the dealings of Providence bring to the unbelieving darkness and despair, while to the trusting soul they are full of light and peace. The path where God leads the way may lie through the desert or the sea, but it is a safe path.
>
> E. G. White, *Patriarchs and Prophets*, p. 290

For the typical believer of the last days the final test will be of the same character as hundreds of preceding ones, only greatly magnified. Every day we encounter tests of the spirit, small and large, but each is intended to prepare us for the final trial. Remember that "a little thing is a little thing, but faithfulness in little things is a great thing."

Balaam and Balak on the Borders of the Promised Land (Numbers 22-24)

Balaam is used in the Apocalypse as the type of the last false prophet (see chapters 3 and 13). He had once been a worshipper of the true God but had apostatized. Yet he still professed faith in the true God and he pretended to serve him. Covetousness destroyed him, but before his death he devised a plan to seduce Israel from fidelity to Yahweh. Read Numbers 22-24. Balaam's union with Balak, the king of Moab, prefigures the final union of apostate religion with the state. His subtlety warns us that in the final test the great Deceiver of the world will pull out all the stops to deceive the people of God. And, tragically, many will fall. Surely we are not safe a moment without leaning on "the everlasting arms." Christ has warned us that without him we can do nothing. Signs and wonders will convince all who rely on sight alone.

Is not the Apocalypse a marvellously written book? Its early chapters are the seed for the later ones. Balaam and Jezebel are shown to have eschatological significance. But the early chapters themselves draw from the garden of the Old Testament. Thus from the beginning of time God foresaw all that was coming. He has ruled and overruled in all challenges to his people so that those who at the end would experience the most severe of trials, a tribulation such as never was, might be encouraged. There are no chance happenings for believers. Accidents are really only incidents, and disappointments should be spelled as Hisappointments.

The Tests in Babylon

Daniel is the book that had most influence on the New Testament. All of Christ's chief teachings about the end times are based on the prophecies of Daniel. From its very first verse the contents of this Old Testament apocalypse are relevant for those living in the last days.

The introduction to Daniel records the onslaught of Babylon, the king of the north, against the holy people and their sacred Temple. We have the same at the end of the book: see Daniel 11:40-45 to 12:7. In New Testament times the names of ancient Israel and his associations are retained but now apply to "the Israel of God"—the Christian church. So, what we have at the close of Daniel is the prediction that Antichrist will attack Christ's people on the eve of his own annihilation.

In chapter two the head of the image is Babylon, but the legs and feet are Roman, pointing to the greater tribulations to be brought upon God's people by pagan and spiritual Rome, and the final Antichrist. Rome ruled the world when John wrote Revelation and became the prototype of the final persecutor—"great Babylon." See Revelation chapters 14-18.

In chapter three where the furnace is heated seven times hotter than normal, we have a symbol of the time of trouble such as never was at the end of history. The three Hebrews, who would not bend, budge, or burn, represent those faithful to Christ in the climactic test of the ages over false worship. The key word "deliver" ("rescue" in some versions) is repeated significantly in Daniel 12:1. While many saints will die enduring the crisis depicted in Revelation 13, others will be delivered by the return of Christ. And those who have died in martyrdom will immediately be raised to life and delivered from lasting death.

In chapter four, the boastful monarch of Babylon is cut down and humbled. So it is to be in the times depicted in Revelation 11-20.

The fifth chapter of Daniel records the overthrow of Babylon when Cyrus and his armies came from the East and diverted the water of the River Euphrates, which ran underneath Babylon. Revelation 16, in the sixth plague, draws upon this ancient overthrow of the persecutor of God's people. Christ will come from the eastern heavens and destroy the "peoples" represented by the raging Euphrates. All this is symbolized by the term Armageddon.

In Daniel six we have the account of a faithful worshipper of God who refused to change his mode of adoration of the true God despite death threats. Here was a liontamer who said his prayers. No accusation against him was true except that he was loyal to the law of his God. While thrown into the den of lions, which was sealed, he emerged unscathed, delivered by the providence of God. So it will be yet again when the saints at the end time are threatened with death if they refuse to change their worship practices. See Revelation 13.

In chapter seven we have a repeat of chapter two with additional information about the final persecutions by Antichrist. The promise is given that the Son of Man will take the kingdom and vindicate his threatened people. Though Antichrist ventures to change the sacred seasons and the law, ultimately the lawgiver will return to avenge truth and truth-keepers.

Chapter eight resumes the Hebrew language because henceforward secular powers are minimized, and the destiny of the saints is enlarged. This chapter is the seedbed of the rest of the book, and of all New Testament eschatology. Antichrist figures largely here. A promise is given of the vindication of all that which is holy (Daniel 8:14), and Daniel 9:24 and 12:1-3 will explain how that promise would be implemented.

Chapter nine is a continuation of the interpretation given Daniel of his previous vision. Verse 24 is the key verse promising the coming of the Messiah and with him the fulfilment of all Old Testament visions and promises. But the counterfeit Messiah—the abomination of desolation is also present in this prophecy with the promise concerning his destruction.

Chapters 10-12 continue to fill out the meaning of the vision of the eighth chapter. Again the abomination of desolation occupies a prominent place in his type—Antiochus Epiphanes—and then in the ultimate reality and antitype, the final Antichrist. The last verses of chapter 11 picture Antichrist sweeping victoriously over the whole world and surrounding the Holy City, the figure of the church. Daniel 11:44 uses a Hebrew term meaning to proscribe or sentence to death. But the following verses promise the deliverance of the faithful remnant simultaneously with the destruction of the abomination of desolation in its concluding manifestation.

Chapter 12 is the epilogue of Daniel and uses some of the same language found in the first chapter such as "days," "stand," and "end." While it tells of the coming onslaught upon the faithful and the death of many, by its promise of resurrection all is made well. The Olivet Discourse, 2 Thessalonians 2, and Revelation enlarge upon all these themes and act as commentary upon them. But Daniel has given us more typical pictures of the end times than the rest of the Old Testament put together.

Esther

Here is an amazing book, which, while it mentions the name of a heathen king over 150 times, does not name God once. But though the divine face is not to be seen, his providential hand is everywhere apparent. This is the most graphic picture of a murderous pogrom so far in the Old Testament. Haman, a figure of Satan and Antichrist, is determined to wipe out the people whose laws are different to the laws of others, and who worship differently in consequence. But providence paved the way for his downfall and he is impaled on a stake—anticipation of the manner in which Christ by his Cross would destroy the real Antichrist—Satan himself. The terrible fate, which overtook Israel's national would-be murderers, typifies the final destruction of the wicked. The law of the harvest is illustrated in all the historical books of Scripture.

The Pattern of Passion Week

It is important to remember that though the story of Christ's ministry is found in the New Testament, the Old Testament era only came to an end when Christ rose from the dead. Until the Cross event, Old Testament laws and customs held sway.

The last days of Christ prefigure the last days of his body—the church. He, at his Triumphal Entry, presented his message and claims as never before, symbolic of the final proclamation of the gospel foretold in Matthew 24:14; Mark 13:10; and Revelation 18:1-4; 10:1,2 and 14:6.

Christ's public presentation of himself led to a polarizing of the people and the final decision of the Jews to have him crucified. Even so will it be when God's people in Pentecostal power give the last proclamation of the everlasting gospel. They will be outlawed, proscribed, and sentenced to death. Indeed, many will be martyred, only to rise in glory shortly afterwards.

Christ was betrayed by one of his own—Judas. The latter is a type of the final Antichrist. He began his career by professing to love Christ, but ended his days by murderous rage against him. In John 12, we find the maturing of love and hate—the gift sponsored by Mary's broken heart (symbol of God's gift on Calvary), and the climactic criticism by Judas. These attitudes typify those of Christ's true disciples in the end time, and also those who apostatize.

Christ had a little time of trouble in Gethsemane, and then his great time of trouble on Calvary. Sentenced to death by the Antichrist of that day he also accepted the "second death" at the hands of his heavenly Father. His people too will know increasing threat and trauma until their power seems absolutely shattered (Daniel 12:7). But as Easter Sunday undid all the trials of Christ, so will the return of Christ and the accompanying resurrection do the same for Christ's people.

Anticipation of "a time of trouble such as never was"—foretold in the Olivet discourse, Daniel 12:1 and Revelation 3:10—cannot but prove disturbing to us. Dwight L. Moody was once asked if he had the courage to be a martyr. Here is his reply: "No, but if God wanted me to be a martyr he would give me the courage."

Devout commentators on Scripture have wrestled with the plain meaning of Daniel 12:7; Revelation 20:4; 13:15; and 11:8. For example, H. C. Leupold has written on Daniel 12:7:

> The solemn news that the holy people must pass through the sad experience of having their power shattered. [The Hebrew term] involves complete demolition of power. Hard though this seems, it is merely one of those necessities to which human pride and self-will put the grace of God before God's gracious purposes can be accomplished. Strangely, man is so set on trusting in himself and depending on his own power that, unless that power is reduced to a helpless minimum, he will refuse to put his confidence wholly in the good Lord. Only after we have been rendered weak are we capable of becoming truly strong. Israel of Old Testament days had to be reduced to the impotence of the last times of the old covenant before the Saviour could come. So her trust in self will have to be broken again before the Christ can return.

Edward J. Young on Daniel 12:1 says:

> We now understand the full sense of this instruction, as the church shall remain in safety amidst many deaths and even in the last stage of despair it shall escape through the help and mercy of God.

And on 12:7 he writes, "The Antichrist will practically have destroyed God's people, when Antichrist himself shall be destroyed." And Joyce G. Baldwin in her commentary writes:

> Suddenly and surely, at the appropriate moment, divine intervention will interrupt history's course. The visible sign of that moment, of interest only to those enduring suffering, is the utter helplessness of believers in the face of their persecutors; thus, paradoxically, when they are enduring the greatest agony of unjust trial and torture they are to look expectantly for the promised intervention of God's deliverance.

C. F. Keil in his commentary on Daniel states:

> The shattering of the hand (Hebrew original of 12:7) is thus the complete destruction of power to work, the placing in a helpless and powerless condition. ... when this state of things shall arise, "then the

Lord shall judge his people, and repent himself for his servants" …
the crushing of the holy people in the tribulation such as never was
before, but also their deliverance by the coming of the angel-prince
Michael, the resurrection of the dead, and the eternal separation of
the righteous from the wicked.

A. Lacoque comments: "When the dismemberment of the power of the holy
people is ended, all these things will come to an end" (his translation of 12:7).
The people will be totally humiliated but the end will be glorious.

These comments remind us of the picture of Jacob after his time of trouble
wrestling with the angel. The text says, "he was limping." We also limp, but,
"when we are weak, then are we strong." See 2 Corinthians 12.

PART TWO

What Is the Everlasting Gospel?

Chapter Eight

What Is the Gospel That Antichrist Hates and Labours to Destroy?

The following pages are of much greater importance than those that have preceded them. Antichrist gains his power over all who have not been captivated by the beauty of God's good news—the Christian gospel. All the alluring temptations of our own day are but substitutes for the real thing—God's love for sinners, and the grace that is willing to declare righteous the most outrageous sinners. (See Romans 4:5 and Luke 6:35.)

Don't let anyone tell you that Christianity and religion are irrelevant. The most significant fact in your existence and mine is that old-fashioned concept called "sin." Human life is happy or unhappy, fruitful or unfruitful, significant or insignificant, because of its relationship not to things, but to this distinctive—are we doing what we know to be right? There's nothing in this world that deals with sin effectively except the gospel!

What makes life matter is friendship, love, fellowship, honesty, purity, and truthfulness. You can't cut them up, parcel them up, and send them through the mail. They are all intangibles. But these are the things that make life significant. Our present existence is characterized by joy or sorrow according to our love relationships with our Creator, our brother, sister, wife, husband, father, mother, children, and the people with whom we work. And only the gospel can make these relationships altogether right. Think of it this way: Primarily we have only three relationships—with ourselves, our neighbour, and our God. Unless we are right with God, we cannot accept ourselves; and if we cannot accept ourselves, we cannot accept our neighbour.

Billy Graham once wrote:

The most terrible and dreadful fact of the universe is the fact of sin. It is the root of all sorrow and the cause of all trouble. It has reversed man's nature. It's robbed him of nobility, brought him down to the dust. It's made him a devil. Sin—it's like a tornado on the loose, like a volcano gone wild. It's like a streak of lightning flashing toward the earth, a madman on the prowl.

Because of this one thing, sin, every life's cup has been made bitter. Because of sin, the light of every day is darkened to some extent. Because of sin, every stream is polluted, every wind that blows is tainted, every prospect is marred, every memory has a sting in it, and every roadway of life is filled with pitfalls. It is the cause of all sorrow and pain, all anguish. This devastating cancer eats at man, this tremendous scourge of evil which is trying to wipe us all out is the reality of life with which the gospel alone deals.

The sin problem dwarfs all other problems by comparison. After finding its solution in the gospel Luther exclaimed, "Strike now, Lord, now my sins are forgiven, do what Thou wilt."

The sin problem subjectively considered has three aspects:

—the guilt of sin
—the power of sin
—the presence of sin.

Theologically these have been dealt with by reference to the Bible's teaching on justification, sanctification, and glorification.

But we need to beware of the error of thinking that the plan of salvation is for man's sake alone. There is an objective aspect, which concerns the whole universe. The New Testament teaches that God had a problem as well as man. Both problems are solved according to Romans 3:26 by Christ's Atonement, which enabled God to be seen as both "just and the justifier" of him who believes in Jesus.

God's problem was to reconcile his position as Judge and Father of the race. How could He uphold his righteous law and yet forgive those who had violated it? How could He be both Light and Love? The New Testament has a strange double picture of God. He is presented as the God who is our heavenly Father without whom not a sparrow falls to the ground. He is also presented as the

Judge who, after he has killed, can destroy the wicked. Even Christ himself is represented as acting with a sternness that cannot be distinguished from that which he attributes to his Father. Yet one of his own parables which sounds very severe is in the immediate context of instruction to his disciples to forgive 70 times 7. See Matthew 18:21-35 and also Matthew 25:31-46. The fact is that God and sin cannot exist together. Not only is it true that in God there is no darkness at all, but also it is impossible for those who walk in darkness to have fellowship with him. Light, then, is holiness, the principle of opposition to sin and separation from it. The only way God could solve his problem was to demonstrate his regard for his law by exacting its penalty and yet to do so in such a way that it would both save man and transform him. Here we have the genius of the Cross.

The Cross of Christ justified the law and the character of God better than if all of the human race had kept every jot and tittle of the law from the time of Adam onwards. Here God took upon himself his own estimate of sin and guilt. But he did so in such a way as to break the heart of man and so free him from the clutches of selfishness which is the essence of law-breaking.

Justification is the most important of the three areas of soteriology (the study of salvation). It concerns the provision of that righteousness alien to us and found in Christ alone. It is systematically presented as a doctrine in Romans, but it is found throughout the whole of Scripture. Even the miracles and parables of Christ set it forth. For example, the leprous, the blind, the deaf, the dumb, and the palsied came just as they were, but the word of Christ declared them whole. They came just as they were, but they did not remain just as they were. Contact with Christ made the difference. His power alone worked the transformation as they submitted to it. In the parables we have the lost pictured as helpless sheep, forfeited coins, and degraded sons. Only loving grace made the rescue possible.

The shepherd found the sheep, the woman found the coin, and the memory of the Father's love drew the prodigal. The prodigal confesses, as must every sinner, "I am not worthy," but the Father receives him none the less. Justification is the reception of the sinner just as he or she is, for Christ's sake. Sanctification or transformation is the result. The essence of justification is that God does for us what we could never do for ourselves. He accomplished our acquittal through Christ's life and death, which were not only substitutionary, but representative. When Christ died, God counted it as though the whole human race died. All he did was put to the credit of the whole human race.

He became what he was not, that we might become what we are not. See 2 Corinthians 5:14,21; and Romans 5:18.

Justification is a declaring righteous, not a making righteous. But the latter is the inevitable consequence of the former. God does not pronounce the leper clean and leave him a leper. He does not pardon the rebel and then leave him to carry on his rebellion. Sanctification begins with regeneration which ever accompanies the faith and penitence which mark justification. Sanctification concerns our state, which is ever imperfect, whereas justification concerns our standing which with God is ever perfect. The "fruit of the Spirit" is the evidence that we have been "born" of the Spirit.

The hand that receives the gift of a perfect standing with God is the hand of faith. The New Testament never says that we are saved because of our faith, but always by means of our faith. Faith has no merit of its own. Its merit is in its object—Christ. Justification by faith means justification by Christ. A trembling hand can receive a golden cup. The story of the woman with the hemorrhage who touched Christ's garment illustrates the nature of saving faith. That faith may be incomplete, superstitious, trembling, and yet if it makes contact with Christ it avails for complete salvation. The destination of heaven is sure for all who have faith, but some travel first class and some travel third class—according to their faith be it unto them. The destination is the same.

Justification can be regarded as the objective aspect of redemption. It is concerned with what has been entirely done outside of us. But the results are subjective. As faith lays hold of the gift of salvation the Holy Spirit which inspires that faith begets a new life in seed form. Henceforth the believer, so to speak, is a person with two natures, the old and the new.

The subjective experience of the one who receives justification is technically called sanctification as has been shown. This has its beginning simultaneously in time but logically in succession to the faith which justifies. We come just as we are but we never remain just as we are.

I would not work my soul to save,
For that the Lord has done,
But I would work like any slave,
For love of God's dear Son.

To run and work the Law commands

But gives me neither feet nor hands.
Better news the gospel brings
It bids me fly and gives me wings.

We do not work to the Cross, but from the Cross. Our actual experiential freedom from sin comes as we bask in the forgiveness of God. Our gratitude and love for God's great gift become a torrent washing away our defilement. As we sense that we are no longer under law, but under grace as regards our acceptance with God, we receive freedom over the habits that have long bound us. But the power of sin is never removed till the guilt of sin has been taken away (Romans 6:14). We come to recognize that the Law is a perfect standard of righteousness, but we acknowledge that it can never give us a perfect standing. The Law is not even a means of sanctification except as it drives us to Christ and indicates what the will of God is. The New Testament shows a decided opposition to law—not to law as a standard, only to law as a method.

The justification I have received covers my past, present, and future. See John 13:10. See also Romans 8:1 and 1 Corinthians 1:30. Christ is even made unto me sanctification. The Christian should not look upon himself as being continually in and out of grace because of his mistakes and failures. He or she is "accepted in the beloved" and "complete in him." Looking to Christ by simple faith, one can never be lost. Christ does not make us robots, and we are free at any time to wilfully pursue a course of deliberate, known sin. This can separate us from him, but we are to remember that though our grasp on him may be feeble, his hold on us is that of an elder brother. Having died for us he will never withdraw from us because we make mistakes.

Romans 5:18 and 2 Corinthians 5:14 show us that when Christ died, it was reckoned as though the whole wicked world died. Henceforth our debts are paid. But our cure experientially is not yet complete. Our way to the kingdom of God may be marked by stumbling, limping, and crawling upon the floor. A Christian of vast experience once wrote: "We ourselves are constantly falling, failing in speech and action to represent Christ, falling and rising again, despairing and hoping." Our holiness is not purely ethical, though it seeks to so be, but rather one that is manifested in an increasing humility and awareness of sinfulness. So the marks of sanctification are not the marks of legalistic achievement, but rather increasing prayerfulness, increasing self-distrust, and increasing faith in him alone who can save and keep. If we do not manifest an increasing hated for our sins, we have never been justified.

Romans 5:1-11 lists some of the aspects of the subjective experience of the believer. Now that justification has come, so has peace, and joy, and love for God. Patience is developed by the manner one reacts to trial, trouble, and tribulation. One grows towards that perfection with which the believer is initially and forever credited. Christ regards us as though the work is already complete. We are already seated in heavenly places in Christ, having died with him, been buried with him, and having risen with him. See Galatians 2:20; Romans 6:4; and Colossians 3:1.

The Christian is admonished to become what he already is. That is, because he is a child of the king, he is to act like one. Therefore at every stage of his experience the Christian may know that he is fully accepted of God, despite his or her internal ups and downs of feelings, emotions, and ethical achievements, or failures. Note that the second half of each Pauline Epistle stresses the "therefore" in the life of the justified. Justification without holiness is a heresy.

First Corinthians 15 describes the final phase of the Plan of Redemption, which is glorification. Only at the coming of the Lord will this lowly body and mind be transformed so that we might become entirely like Christ. The chimera of sinlessness in this life is not a New Testament hope. Romans 7:14-25 and Galatians 5:17 show that the flesh strives against the spirit continually. Sin remains, but it should not reign. The Christian is able not to sin, but he is not unable to sin. In essence, as Luther said, "The Christian is always a sinner, always a penitent, and always right with God."

For practical Christian living, the challenge is to focus our attention on what Christ is to us rather than what we are to him. We are not to make the mistake of reasoning from feeling to fact to faith, but the reverse. God's love and acceptance of us is like the blaze of the sun, ever complete and full and warm. But our attitude to God is like that of the waning moon, ever incomplete, and ever but a slight reflection of his own. Objectively in redemption, Christ is all. However, subjectively, faith is all. No one will ever perish while he or she depends upon the merits of the Atonement. But any professed Christian who regards sin lightly has never accepted the Atonement.

The two ills doctrinally in the matter of salvation are those of legalism and antinomianism. The former teaches that we must be good in order to be saved. The latter teaches that being saved, we can do as we like. Both these are erroneous. God accepts us just as we are. The legalism in the New Testament was not the belief that we are saved by works, but that we are saved by faith and works. In reality, we are saved by faith alone, though the faith that saves is never alone.

We are not saved by faith and works, but by faith that works. Neither does sanctification come by looking to self. There we find only insufficiency, inadequacy, and sin. We are saved by looking to the Saviour. For every look at the wound of sin, give ten to the great Physician. Whatever gets our attention gets us. Whatever we hold in the mind passes into action. If the Christian continually keeps his sin and failures and mistakes in his mind, he will sin and make mistakes more and more. But if Christ is preeminent in the Christian's thinking, then he will grow more and more like his Master—"looking unto Jesus the author and finisher of our faith." "We all with open face beholding as in mirror the glory of the Lord are changed into the same image from glory to glory" (Heb. 12:2; 2 Cor. 3:18).

"Christ received is holiness begun. Christ cherished is holiness advancing. Christ counted upon as never absent would be holiness complete."

Chapter Nine

The Nature and Importance of Justification

However long we have been Christians and however thoroughgoing we are, to trust in our own inherent righteousness is the worst of folly. The infinite Law of God (Psalm 119) demands a perfect nature, perfect thoughts, perfect emotions, perfect motives, perfect words, and perfect deeds. Only sinless beings, fully controlled by the Holy Spirit from their first breath to their last, can fulfil that Law. In justification the infinite righteousness of Christ, the God-man—is imputed to us. Our sins were imputed to him in order that his righteousness might therefore be reckoned to us (2 Corinthians 5:21). It is vital that we fully comprehend what the Scriptures teach upon this primary doctrine. The first five chapters of the first of the New Testament Epistles are dedicated to it, and allusions to it are found throughout all of Scripture. Let us look at some of the biblical references.

There are at least a dozen or so metaphors used in the New Testament for Christ's saving work. Propitiation is used 4 times, redemption 11, ransom 3, and reconciliation 5. The only image used over and over again is the legal metaphor of justification. The Greek term with its cognates occurs approximately 230 times in the New Testament. Compare it with the others mentioned. It should be kept in mind that "justification" and "righteousness" are translations of the same Greek word. This, of course, means that "righteousness by faith" in the New Testament is exactly the same as "justification by faith." Sanctification is no part of it, but always results from it. Scholars are agreed that justification is primary in Paul's theology. No Christian can have a fully-orbed understanding of what Christ has done without comprehending what Paul taught on this subject.

Justify

In both the Old and the New Testaments (and the LXX) the words translated "justify" signify "to declare righteous," not "to make righteous" (except in a judicial sense). Linguists and lexicons usually describe these words as "forensic," i.e., having a legal connotation associated with law, judgment, and judges. See any dictionary, secular or religious.

Luther, Calvin, Wesley, Whitefield, Jonathan Edwards, and Spurgeon influenced millions and changed the course of history because they affirmed that the essence of the gospel was the glorious truth that, because our sin was imputed to Christ and he suffered accordingly, his righteousness is imputed to the believer, and we will be ultimately with him in glory. See Romans 1:16-17; 3:20-38; 4:6-8; 5:1-21; 8:1,33-34; Galatians 1:6-9; 2:16,19-21; 3:10-13; 6:14; l Corinthians 1:30; 6:11; Philippians 3:9; Luke 18:9-14; 2 Corinthians 5:14-21, etc.

Conspectus of the Traditional View Proclaimed by Protestant Leaders

Their stress was ever upon Romans 4:5 about the God who "justifies the wicked." Their often-repeated emphasis was the fact that the believer is accounted 100 per cent righteous, though he or she is still a sinner by nature. Justification is the opposite of condemnation. To condemn does not mean to make bad, and to justify does not mean to make good. The righteousness of justification is one hundred percent, but it is outside of us and is only reckoned to us, whereas the righteousness of sanctification is never one hundred per cent, but it is inside us because of the work of the indwelling Holy Spirit. This sanctification is the work of a lifetime and is never complete until glorification at the return of our Lord. Thus believers must rely on their justification and not their sanctification, although it remains true that God justifies none whom he does not sanctify. The two blessings are distinct, but never separate. Despite continuing failures, the believer's sins are not reckoned against him or her. See Romans 4:8. While a course of premeditated wilful sin can separate the believer from Christ, a million shortcomings cannot. Calvary covers all our sins, past, present, and future.

Traditionally some small Protestant groups have understood "righteousness by faith" to include justification and sanctification, thus showing ignorance of the Greek New Testament and reaping a void of assurance. The English words "righteousness" and "justification" come from the same Greek term, and righteousness by faith means justification by faith and nothing more, although its fruit is always holy living.

Sanctification is not downgraded by the New Testament gospel. See the second half of each Pauline Epistle and 1 Corinthians 6:9-11 and Romans 6 in particular. But it must be kept in mind that the biblical use of the term sanctification and the theological use are not identical as regards terminology. In Scripture "to sanctify" usually means "to set apart." The theological, more popular meaning, has to do with growth in grace under the influence of the Holy Spirit.

Consider the following verses that use "justify." All of them make plain that the term signifies an accounting or imputing of righteousness, not an imparting. Modern versions often use "acquit." Particularly observe how now in New Testament times, because of Christ's atonement on the Cross, God can do what in Old Testament times he declared he could not do. See Exodus 23:7; Deuteronomy 25:1; Isaiah 5:22-23; 2 Chronicles 6:23; Proverbs 17:15; Matthew 12:37; Luke 7:29,35; Luke 10:29; Romans 2:13,16; and Romans 3:4.

Evangelical believers have never given "justify" any other meaning than "declare righteous." Wesley clearly states that justification is not the new birth, nor the process of sanctification, and that his understanding was the same as that of Luther and Calvin.

Scholarly Works on *Dikaiow* (Greek for "justify")

One of the greatest scholars of the last century wrote the following:

> There is hardly an exegete of the first rank who will dispute that in Paul's usage the word *dikaiow*, "to justify," is employed uniformly in the sense of absolving, acquitting, declaring righteous before the law, and can never bear the sense of making righteous—is used, in short, in the "forensic" sense, as the opposite of "to condemn," and that the ground of that absolving sentence is not "works of righteousness," or incipient holiness, in the person justified, but "the redemption that is in Christ Jesus, whom God set forth to be a propitiation, through faith, in his blood."

James Orr, *The Progress of Dogma,* pp. 259-260

The most well known comment on this topic among scholars comes from Schrenk in the *Theological Dictionary of the New Testament* on *dikaiow*:

> In Paul the legal use is plain and indisputable. ... For Paul the word *dikiouw* does not suggest the infusion of moral qualities. ... It implies the justification of the ungodly who believe, on the basis of the justifying action of God in the death and resurrection of Christ.

Vol. 2, p. 215

Frederick Godet in his *Commentary on Romans*: "as to *dikaiow*, there is not an example in the whole of classic literature where it signifies to make just." (Leon Morris cites it on page 157 as a footnote to his page 252, but this must be an early edition.)

See C. E. B. Cranfield, Leon Morris, and George Eldon Ladd, etc. Even James D. G. Ladd (the baptizer of the New Perspective on Paul and whose general view in support of Sanders departs from the traditional), states in *Romans,* volume 1, 153: "The verb used for a final verdict, not excluding the idea of the final verdict at the end of a life." ... "It is clear enough that Paul can think of righteousness as a gift, a potency or status or relationship received from God" (p. 295).

N. T. Wright, the most popular exponent of the NPP, whose distinctive views diverge from traditional ones, says: "Justification ... is organically and integrally linked to ... the Gospel" (cited by Paul Barnett, *Romans: The Revelation of God's Righteousness,* p. 17).

F. F. Bruce in his *Commentary on Romans* has on page 38 a footnote, agreeing in essence with what has been cited above. But he also, by a pertinent quotation, makes a very practical application of justification that should be of real interest to all members of the laity desirous of church reform:

> Justification by Faith means that salvation depends not on sacraments, not on what is done or not done by any priest or presbyter, but on the simple response of the believing heart to the Word of God in Jesus Christ. Observe what this really means; it is not just a theological figment. At one stroke it cuts at the root of the whole vast system of sacerdotalism, with its associated works—penance, pilgrimage, fasting, purgatory, and all the rest. The church is no longer a hierarchy of clergy performing indispensable rites for its

members; no longer a caste of priests endowed with mysterious, not to say magical powers at the word of a bishop; but the priesthood of all believing men, and a ministry authorized by the call of the Holy Spirit, by due examination of life and doctrine, and by the consent of the people concerned. Accept this doctrine of Justification by Faith and the layman, the common man, John the Commonweal, at one stride comes into the centre.

Then Bruce adds:

> The doctrine of justification by faith underlies and undergirds the forms which democracy has taken in those lands most deeply influenced by the Reformation; it is a bastion of true freedom. Luther was charged with "inciting revolution by putting little people in mind of their prodigious dignity before God." How could he deny the change? The gospel, as he had learned it from Paul, does precisely that.

> *Romans*, pp. 39-40

Martin Chemnitz, *Examination of the Council of Trent,* volume 1, page 476, states:

> But it must be diligently considered why the Holy Spirit wanted to set forth the doctrine of justification by means of juridical terms. Worldly, secure, and Epicurean men think that the justification of the sinner is something easy and perfunctory, therefore they are not much concerned about sin and do not sincerely seek reconciliation with God, nor do they strive with any diligence to retain it. However, the peculiar nature of the word "justify" shows how weighty and serious an action before the judgment seat of God the justification of a sinner is. Likewise, the human mind, inflated with a Pharisaical persuasion when it indulges in its own private thoughts concerning righteousness, can easily conceive a high degree of confidence and trust in its own righteousness. But when the doctrine of justification is set forth under the picture of an examination and of the tribunal of divine judgment, by a court trial, so to say, those Pharisaical persuasions collapse, vanish, and are cast down.

The classics R. W. Dale's *The Atonement*, and James Denney's *The Death of Christ* (which transformed the ministry of Martyn Lloyd-Jones and thousands of other preachers) should be studied to see the relationship between the Cross and justification.

See also *Great Controversy*, p. 256; *Steps to Christ*, p. 79, and 1 *Selected Messages,* pp. 395-367, by Ellen G. White.

Paul himself explains justification (set forth in Romans 3:21-28) in Romans 4 by the eleven-fold use of "impute" or "reckon."

When we consider the depths of the divine law and the remaining depravity of the best of believers it is clear that unless Christ's own merits can be declared as ours by imputation we have no hope of surviving the judgment. That's why this topic is "the one interest that should prevail, the one subject that should swallow up every other, the sweetest melody from human lips—the Lord our Righteousness."

Chapter Ten

Counterfeits of the New Testament Gospel: Legalism, Antinomianism, the Moral Influence Theory

Legalism

Satan is the great counterfeiter. This is shown in Revelation chapter 13. Counterfeiting God and his gospel is part of the subtlety of the great adversary. He hates the Cross which sealed his doom, and for centuries he has laboured to destroy its significance.

All informed Christians know that legalism is a heresy, but too often it is interpreted as meaning a bald salvation by works. The more widespread and subtler form of this heresy is the conjoining of faith and works to make the doer acceptable to God. This was the medieval understanding of justification, against which Luther and Calvin protested. It is a form of semi-pelagianism whereby grace is truncated, and man's efforts are given a credit not truly available to depraved and fallen beings. The majority of professed Christians have been trapped by this fallacy and depend in part upon their own goodness to attain acceptance with God. When sanctification is given a priority over justification this heresy is implemented. Often it paves the way for yet another heresy—perfectionism. Romans 6:14; 7:14-25; and Ephesians 2:8-10 were written to save believers from these deceptions.

The Epistles of Galatians and Romans also reject this heresy, as Christ himself had done by parable after parable, and pronouncement after pronouncement. See particularly Luke chapter 18, the pharisee and the publican, and Matthew 20, the parable of the labourers. Observe that in the former parable, the pharisee did give God some credit yet simultaneously looked chiefly at his own "goodness." But it is not enough to thank God for his grace while depending chiefly on our own efforts. The second parable reminds us that we are not to put faith in either the quality or quantity of our "good works." Everything we do is tainted with sin, and mixed motives govern all that we do.

Antinomianism

Far less common is antinomianism, the teaching that grace makes obedience unnecessary. The second half of the chief Epistles of Paul reject this with hundreds of verses. "If ye love me, keep my commandments," is a phrase from Christ which no true believer can ignore.

The Moral Influence Theory

The moral influence theory is very popular today, even making ground in evangelical churches. It teaches that the death of Christ was not a sacrifice, but only a revelation of the love of God. It is right in what it affirms, and wrong in what it denies. It makes ignorance rather than sin the chief problem in the world. Because the world is ignorant of God's love, sin prevails.

There are great problems with this view. First of all, the New Testament does not teach it. Look at the third chapter of Romans or the third of Galatians or Ephesians 2—these classic passages on redemption know nothing of this theory. Furthermore, it makes the Cross of no avail to all who lived before Christ. They did not know of the tide of reconciling love revealed at Calvary. Third, the passages rejoicing in the atoning blood of Christ and his sacrifice for us are too numerous to pass by.

R. W. Dale wrote his great classic, *The Atonement,* to show the biblical evidence for the objective nature of Christ's atonement. He was deeply troubled by the spread of the moral influence theory. Note his words:

> The fundamental question, whether the death of Christ has a direct relation to the remission of sins, or whether it was simply a great appeal of the Divine love to the human heart … determines the whole attitude of the Christian soul to Christ. One of these two conceptions we must accept, one we must reject, not merely as theologians, but as Christians. One of these two theories is implicated in every devotional act, in every confession of sin, in every prayer for forgiveness, in every thanksgiving for redemption.
> *The Atonement,* pp. 10-11

When the same author discusses Galatians 3:13 ("Christ redeemed us from the curse of the law by becoming a curse for us"), he comments as follows:

> Try, if you can, to remove from that passage the idea that Christ endured the penalty of the law—the curse—in order that those who had transgressed the law might be redeemed from the curse and inherit the promise. Make the Death of Christ an appeal to the hearts and consciences of men, and let there be nothing in it which can be described as a vicarious endurance of penalty, and what becomes of the whole structure of the Apostle's argument? ... the Death of Christ is the ground on which sins are remitted, and it effected an objective Atonement for sin

Ibid., p. 222

After his discussion of the first few chapters of Romans, Dale engages with the moral influence subjective theory of the death of Christ:

> But in those passages of the epistle which immediately follow the declaration of the universal guilt of mankind, is there anything to suggest that the Apostle's mind was occupied with the spiritual influences which now act on the heart and conscience of the race—anything to suggest that Christ delivers men from the Divine wrath solely because He changes their dispositions and character; and that by the normal action of "spiritual laws" men gradually escape from the consequences of sin, as through Christ they are gradually attracted and disciplined to holiness? ... When St. Paul speaks of "the righteousness of God which is by faith in Jesus Christ," it is possible to suppose that he is thinking of that subjective change which is the result of faith in Christ—a change by which man recovers the image of the Divine holiness. The ambiguity may not disappear when he speaks of our "being justified freely by his grace through the redemption that is in Christ Jesus"; but the words which immediately follow, and the contents of the next few pages of the epistle, are an irresistible proof that as yet St. Paul had no thought of the moral and spiritual regeneration which Christ effects in those who believe in Him. He closes his statement of the method by which we are to escape the Divine condemnation before he illustrated either the necessity of ceasing to sin, or the spiritual powers by which our escape from sin is effected.

> At present he is wholly absorbed in the question, how are we to be delivered—not from sin—but from guilt, and from the wrath of God, to which our guilt exposes us?
> *Ibid.,* pp. 233-234

> The Death of Christ is represented—not as the method by which God touches the human heart—but as the ground on which God cancels human guilt, and delivers the guilty from "the wrath" which threatens them.
> *Ibid.,* pp. 236

Dale later points out that the question of Romans 6:1 would have been impossible, if the preceding chapters had been discussing the means by which holiness was restored to the sinner. Then comes his climax:

> Reject the idea of an objective Atonement and of an objective Justification founded upon it, and you must not only strain to unnatural and impossible meanings, words, phrases, and whole sentences in which these ideas are conspicuously present; you must do violence to the plan and structure of nearly the whole of the first half of the epistle. The statement in the first two chapters of the grounds on which the intervention of Christ was necessary is inappropriate; the critical declaration in the third chapter, that Christ has been set forth as a "propitiation … in His blood," is misleading; the conclusion of the argument in the early verses of the fifth chapter, that "being justified by faith we have peace with God," is premature; the necessity for discussing the question at the opening of the sixth chapter "Shall we continue in sin that grace may abound?" is unintelligible; and the discussion which extends through the sixth and seventh chapters lies far remote from the most direct and decisive reply with which the question might have been met. These seven chapters, if every other passage in his epistles were doubtful, would constitute a sufficient and impregnable demonstration that St. Paul believed in an objective Atonement.
> *Ibid.,* p. 249

The moral influence theory is a nest of fallacies, though its chief point that the Cross reveals the love of God is clearly true. It errs by making this the sole meaning of the Cross despite the nearly 600 references to the wrath of God (or synonymous expressions) in Scripture. The theory sets up straw men, making the Trinity divisible and the Law an artificial construct of God rather than his nature. It has Christ save us from sin and only then from penalty, the reverse of the biblical teaching. It considers that all punishment is for purposes of reform and excludes the idea of retribution. It belittles all the passages that speak of wrath, propitiation, reconciliation, Christ being made sin, Christ becoming a curse, etc. It belittles the holiness of God which, according to Scripture, demands that the just demands of the Law should be met. The sacrificial language of the New Testament is ignored, for example Ephesians 5:2, Hebrews 9:14,23,26; and 10:10,12,14,19.

This heresy makes the Cross an unnecessary event as though a friend jumped into the sea in order to drown to prove his love for his companion sitting safely on the shore. The dimensions of the Calvary event are passed by. Nearly half of John's Gospel is devoted to Passion Week, and about a third of the other Gospels. But Paul's death is not even recorded, and one sentence is given to the martyrdom of James. There was no Philippians 1:23 for Jesus, only for Paul. For Christ we have the agony expressed in John 12:27. Why was the veil not torn at the giving of the Sermon on the Mount? Why only when Christ expired? The ordinances of the Christian church commemorate his death. Any teaching which fails to make that sacrifice central is not Christian.

The moral influence theory is based on false principles. It makes the law something arbitrary rather than the very expression of the nature of God. It sees the purpose of penalty only to work reformation. It considers righteousness to be only benevolence. And it is based on a pelagian view of sin, minimizing its abysmal depths. Sin becomes a slight evil and therefore man can save himself. The theory contradicts plain statements from Scripture about objective guilt and it gives no real explanation for the death of Christ. It elevates subordinate effects of the Cross to a position of primacy. It makes Christ's sufferings and death the cost of the Atonement rather than the Atonement itself. It denies that the blood accomplished something for us despite many texts to the contrary. It denies that justification is a pronouncing just as a result of the imputation of Christ's merits enshrined in his life and death. It confines the influence of the Cross to those who have heard of it, despite such passages as John 10:15; John 3:14; and Matthew 26:28. The plain teaching in Holy Writ that the Cross made possible a change of attitude of God towards sinners is ignored. (It was because of his love that God gave his Son, but only because of that event was it right to forgive sinners. See Romans 3:24-26; and 2 Corinthians 5:14-21.)

As is usual for John Stott, he goes to the very core of this issue in his book *The Cross of Christ*. He gives three reasons why the theory is untenable. The first is that those who hold it tend not to take it seriously themselves. Incompatible texts are passed by. Dr H. Rashdall, a chief proponent of the view under consideration, wrote that our belief in biblical inspiration must not prevent us from "boldly rejecting any formulae which seem to say that sin cannot be forgiven without a vicarious sacrifice." John Stott continues:

> We need to quote against Abelard and Rashdall the words of Anselm, "you have not yet considered the seriousness of sin." The 'moral influence' theory offers a superficial remedy because it has made a superficial diagnosis.... It entirely lacks the profound biblical understanding of man's radical rebellion against God, of God's wrath, his outraged antagonism to human sin, and of the indispensable necessity of a satisfaction for sin, which satisfies God's own character of justice and love. James Orr was right that Abelard's "view of atonement is defective precisely on the side on which Anselm's was strong," namely in his analysis of sin, wrath, and satisfaction.

"Third," says Stott, "the moral influence theory has a fatal flaw in its own central emphasis":

> The question we desire to press is this: just how does the cross display and demonstrate Christ's love? What is there in the cross, which reveals love? True love is purposive in its self-giving; it does not make random or reckless gestures.... Paul and John saw love in the cross because they understood it respectively as a death for sinners (Rom. 5:8) and as a propitiation for sin (1 John 4:10). That is to say, the cross can be seen as a proof of God's love only when it is at the same time seen as a proof of his justice."

The Cross of Christ, pp. 219-220

Chapter Eleven

The New Perspective on Paul

The New Perspective on Paul (NPP) is the title given to recent theories, which unite in rejecting traditional understanding of the Apostle and of justification. World War II and its holocaust brought about such revulsion in English and American theologians that many of them damned the Reformers for Anti-Semitism. But Luther, even when most angry with the people who refused the gospel, never urged physical violence against them. For the most part the NPP is taken seriously only in English-speaking countries, where its impact has been considerable. But in the last few years, a strong reaction has come from the evangelical presses, and the insistence that only the Reformation view of Paul's understanding of salvation is exegetically defensible.

So we are moving now to this more recent phenomenon in New Testament scholarship. In the last 40 years we must recognize that there has been a Copernican revolution in Pauline studies. The men who have initiated it are fine scholars, but like their commentators they are men who dare not claim infallibility. If you study what is known as the New Perspective on Paul, you need to keep in mind that, "while all that's old is not pure gold, what is new is rarely true." "He who marries the Spirit of the Age soon becomes a widower." Therefore one needs to recognize that the critical research for the historical Jesus has now opted to search for the real Paul, but its fruitage will be similarly minuscule.

The new emphasis seeks to classify the studies of the last five centuries as antiquated and urges that traditional views on justification should be dropped. It narrows the gap between Paul and the Jews of his day and widens the gap between Paul and the Reformers of the 16th century. Only in the last decade or so have evangelicals recovered their breath and addressed this issue with great carefulness and thoroughness. There is now a spate of scholarly works rebutting the principal claims of the NPP and probably the latter will gradually die.

The NPP scholars are not agreed among themselves, and it is often the case that one leading scholar repudiates the position or positions of another. Only in English speaking countries have the new ideas shown virility and even there are many dissidents. The latter are not to be minimized as they include such giants as F. F. Bruce, Joseph Fitzmeyer, and C. Cranfield.

The new wave began with Krister Stendahl, a Harvard theologian noted not only for his sense of humour, but for his capacity to stir the theological waters. He insisted that Paul was not at all as evangelicals usually pictured him, especially Augustine and Luther. According to Stendahl, Luther had a very robust conscience and was not deeply troubled by a need for gospel balm. Paul's chief concern was about the bringing in of the Gentile believers to a safe haven in the new church. See his book *Paul Among Jews and Gentiles*. His theology is now recognized by many as inadequate and against the historical and biblical evidence.

The following decade, a new star appeared on the theological horizon. It was E. P. Sanders who affirmed vigorously that the Jews of Paul's day were not legalists but devoted to belief in the grace of God. *Paul and Palestinian Judaism* was his magnum opus. With apparent thoroughness he evoked from Jewish literature innumerable statements to the effect that the grace of God was the cause of salvation, not legalistic works.

Sanders rejected many beliefs evangelicals hold dear, such as the deity of Christ and the Virgin birth. But he was followed by a very significant figure, James D. G. Dunn, who commended Sanders in part but rejected certain of his prominent positions. He asserts that Sanders began with a bang but ended with a whimper. Dunn declared he preferred the Paul of the Reformers to the strange figure offered by Sanders. Dunn is also regarded by evangelicals as a liberal, because of his rejection of certain basic traditional teachings. But none can deny his scholarly ability. Listening to the cascade of criticism that came his way, Dunn changed some of his positions setting forth his reconsidered viewpoint in a later book. He taught that justification does not describe how one becomes a member of the people of God but rather is an affirmation that the believer is already accepted in the Christian church.

Dunn put stress upon sociology and saw Paul's concerns as lying chiefly in that area, especially the instance of Christian Jews versus believing Gentiles. He denied that Paul was protesting against legalism in general and suggested that the apostle' antagonism to Jewish practice lay only in the area of circumcision, food laws, and Sabbath-keeping. Many later scholars see such views as unsustainable. For example, there is not one verse that conjoins these three practices and clearly Paul's warnings against "brownie points" from law-keeping involved obedience to moral laws. While Dunn acknowledges that Galatians 3:10-13 is the litmus test of his sociological approach, according to published articles by N. H. Young, his various attempts at passing the test have been unsuccessful.

The most recent theologian in the NPP succession is N. T. Wright. But he is a "different kettle of fish" for he is known for his strong espousal of many evangelical positions. His exegesis of Isaiah 53 has won general acclaim among evangelicals, and likewise much else that he has written. But now many are having second thoughts about Wright, for he too has rejected the traditional Protestant view of justification. He contends that the latter is not so much a "declaring righteous" as "declaring Christian." There he is very close to Dunn, and indeed can be said to be building both on Sanders and Dunn, though not in any slavish fashion.

It is important to recognize that while both Dunn and Wright have severely criticized positions of Martin Luther, neither gives evidence of having looked closely at the original sources. Historians have criticized them both for relying upon secondary opinions some of which are now known to be false. Dunn, for example, teaches that Luther considered Romans 7 as NOT applying to the mature Paul. This is contrary to the historical evidence. In one place Luther gives 10 reasons why Romans 7 does fit the apostle.

Wright's popular book, *What Saint Paul Really Said,* puts a number of things between the acceptance of the gospel and justification. Incorporation into the church by baptism is one of these. For Wright, justification can never be made central.

An increasing number of protests now stress that it is not biblical to see justification as merely a device for finding a place for Gentiles. (Paul in Romans gives more space to the needs of the Jews.) In Romans 1, Paul is emphatic that once the gospel has been heard and accepted, the believer is immediately right with God. One cannot read Romans chapters 1-5 without recognizing that justification is the immediate answer for the believer to the problems of personal guilt, God's wrath against sin, and the Judgment. He who is "righteous by faith" immediately lives with the awareness that he or she has the verdict of the Last Judgment already and possesses eternal life now. See Romans 1:16,17; 3:21-28; 5:1; and 10:9-13.

Wright holds other key positions that do not stand the test of thorough exegesis. He sees the curse of Galatians 3:13 as the curse of the exile. But such is nowhere in the context, whereas dereliction of the law is. N. H. Young and others have criticized this position ably.

Sanders, Dunn, and Wright seem unaware that Luther was not fighting pelagianism but semi-pelagianism, a much more subtle and greater danger. In his conclusions about the documents of the Second Temple Sanders does not indicate that he knows the difference. Recent volumes have shown that Judaism in the years before Christ was immersed in semi-pelagianism, not a bald legalism. "Covenantal nomism" is the name given by Sanders and his successors to the principle of staying in the covenant of God by obedience. But this is what both Paul and Luther rejected. When Wright accuses the Reformers of presenting first century Judaism as pelagian he is wrong. Unwittingly Sanders actually supports the argument of the Reformers.

C. K. Barrett has rightly said that, "He is a bold man who thinks he understands first century Judaism better than Paul." But this is the mistake of most proponents of the NPP. They claim that distorted views of Judaism have led to distorted interpretations of Paul, and that the great Reformers all misunderstood Paul and the battle he was fighting. But in trying to lift from the Jews the burden of legalism, the burden of racism has been substituted.

When Dunn and others insist that Paul's war against the wrong use of law is directed only to "the boundary markers," which distinguished the Jews, they have undertaken an exegetical task, which only turns against them. Interestingly, Dunn never quotes Philippians 3:9 in his chief book *Jesus, Paul and the Law*, yet it is this verse which makes it very clear that Paul's main concern was NOT the boundary markers. Dunn also neglects Romans 4:5; 11:6; and Ephesians 2:8-10.

The main protagonists of the NPP have recently come under very heavy criticism and probably will never recover from it. Wright says of Sanders that he had his own agenda from a modernist comparative religion perspective rather than from a classical theological one (*What Saint Paul Really Said*, p. 20). Ben Witherington (*The Indelible Image*) shows that Sanders has overplayed his hand—for there was no monolithic covenantal nomism view in early Judaism that characterized all Jewish thinking about law. See 4 Ezra, 2 Enoch, 2 and 3 Baruch, and Jubilees. Cranfield says that Dunn's arguments on works are "unconscionably tortuous." See *Journal for the Study of the*

New Testament, Vol. 43, 1991, p. 92. Philip Alexander has issued cautions regarding the use of rabbinic sources and given several reasons for his caveat. He says "It is extremely difficult to lay down a norm for Judaism in the first century." (See his 1999 essay on Jews and Christians in *The Parting of the Ways A.D. 70-135.)*

In *Christianity Today*, August 2007, Cambridge Professor Simon Gathercole summarizes the reasons for rejecting the main positions of the NPP. Frank Thielman in his *From Plight to Solution* has demonstrated Sanders' quite selective use of Palestinian sources. Thielman uses the same sources, but comes to a different conclusion. Moo's *Commentary on Romans* claims that "In passage after passage in his scrutiny of the Jewish literature Sanders dismisses 'a legalistic' interpretation by arguing that the covenant framework must be read into the text, or that the passage is homiletical, rather than theological."

Douglas Wilson says that many of the NPP academics are "theologically brilliant, but pastorally naïve" and he adds, "We must affirm that the gospel is the answer to THE universal human problem which is self-righteousness." See also the work of Carl Trueman, Kim Riddleharger, and Lee Tatiss—historians who fault the NPP. (See the Internet for such articles.)

What is at stake? I quote another, whose name I have lost. "Everything, the purity of the gospel, the remedy for sin, correct theology. If we are wrong here we are wrong everywhere. Forensic justification means sola fide—grace, sheer, unalloyed, unmerited grace. To include the renewing work of the Holy Spirit as justification is to commit blasphemy and to make the Holy Spirit an Antichrist. The comfort of troubled consciences is at stake. Who can look at his own experience and consider he prays enough, loves enough, lives as unselfishly as strict and perfect justice demand. We must not confuse our acceptance with our spiritual attainment."

Amen, say I.

(Recommended for further study: Stephen Westerholm's *Perspectives Old and New on Paul* and *Justification and Variegated Nomism*, vols. 1 & 2, (eds) D.A. Carson; Peter T. O'Brien, Mark A. Seifrid.) For a popular easy-to-read book, not on the NPP but on the gospel as set forth in Romans, see Desmond Ford, *Right With God Right Now*, available through Good News Unlimited.)

Chapter 12

The Atonement

The gospel and its chief metaphor—justification—have their source in the Cross of Christ and his Atonement. We cannot be right about the first two unless correct in our understanding of the latter two. Most cheap modern gospels (especially those heard over television) fail here.

The death of the incarnate Son of God is the most remarkable event in all history. And there is no subject for thought more important than the Atonement of Christ.

The first four books of the New Testament are about the Atonement and so is the first of the Epistles. The rest of the New Testament assumes it and frequently refers to it, using a variety of metaphors. The Gospels have been called passion stories with extended introductions. Half of John's Gospel is about Passion Week, and so is about a third of the other Gospels.

D. E. H. Nineham has this to say about the first Gospel written—Mark:

> Not only has Mark given to the passion the position of pre-eminence and climax in the Gospel—he has so selected and arranged the rest of his material that, for all its importance, it is seen to be subordinate to what happened in Jerusalem. If you read the earlier part of the Gospel attentively, you will see that practically everything in it is in some way introductory to the passion of Jesus; the aim throughout is quite single-minded to help the reader to see Jesus on the Cross.
>
> *Theology*, pp. lx, 269, cited by Leon Morris, *The Cross in the New Testament*, pp. 14-15

Consider the dynamic sentence of Paul, "I determined not to know anything among you save Jesus Christ and him crucified" (1 Corinthians 2:2, KJV).

Who is this being who to Paul is greater than Gabriel and all angels and deserving of constant attention? It is none other than God the Son who died for us to roll away our guilt and energize us in righteousness.

We should contrast the ease of creation as intimated by Genesis chapter one with the cost of redemption. See Christ kneeling in Gethsemane, near to death, as one who has seen some terrible apparition which freezes the blood and paralyses the nerves. Hear him cry on Calvary, "My God, my God, why hast thou forsaken me?" The naked, quivering body is hidden from sight by the darkening of the sun, but his mind and heart also are without a single ray of light. His immaculate purity sensitized him to the slightest manifestation of evil, and in the Passion he is infinitely tormented by the rebel race he loved so much.

Even the Old Testament, written centuries before, offers a trail of blood and tears from Genesis to Malachi, and at its heart we hear the terrible cries of Lamentations, "Is it nothing to all you who pass by? Look around and see. Is there any suffering like my suffering that was inflicted on me, that the Lord brought on me in the day of his fierce anger?" (1:12). In the prophecy of Isaiah 52:13 to 53:1-12, there are 12 precise and explicit statements about the sufferer bearing the penalty of the sins of others. Like Psalm 22, the psalm of sobs, this prophecy sears the mind of the sensitive reader. And day by day at the Jewish temple there was enacted constant death and shedding of blood.

While Scripture has many pictures and metaphors about the Atonement, it never pretends to explain its depths. The thousands of books written on the subject likewise admittedly fall short. The subject is infinite. "The well is deep and we have nothing to draw with." Key terms like substitution, representation, penalty, satisfaction, expiation, propitiation, and reconciliation, etc., help us, but none of them "touch bottom."

Peter Green's meditation on Calvary brought forth these words as he contemplated the cry of dereliction:

> Suppose He had paid all the rest of the price of sin, the suffering, the submission and breaking of pride, and the hatred of sin, and left this unpaid, would it not have been as if He had paid the farthings, pence, and shillings of some vast debt but left the pounds for us to pay?

> *Studies in the Cross*, p. 81

In other words, as Leon Morris points out, "The worst part of the punishment of sin is the cutting off of the sinner from God. The cry of dereliction shows that the price of sin has been paid in full" (*The Cross in the New Testament*, p. 44).

> "Bearing sin and suffering rude
> In my place condemned he stood,
> Sealed my pardon with his blood,
> Hallelujah! What a Saviour!"

A. T. Pierson, who preached at the Metropolitan Tabernacle after the death of Spurgeon, also lectured at Exeter Hall, London. On one occasion he had this to say as he proclaimed the Atonement made at the Cross (we quote at length, for the written record is hard to come by):

> Some of the problems that confronted God with regard to man's redemption we can scarcely understand at all, because of sensibilities dulled by habitual contact with evil. Familiarity with sin involves the loss of all true conception of its enormity and deformity. Yet there can be no high value placed upon the work of Christ until there is some apprehension of the desperation and degradation of man's fallen state, and the utter depravity of his nature.
>
> There are several aspects of sin, which, obviously, must be considered and met in a redemptive plan.... Sin is transgression, and transgression demands penalty. Sin is guilt, and guilt demands expiation. Sin is character, and character demands renewal. Sin is slavery, and slavery demands emancipation. Sin is ruin, and ruin demands rebuilding. Sin is war against Almighty God, and this demands the vindication of God's honour and holiness. There must be on his part no complicity with sin, in a lax fashion of pardoning.

Pierson then offers appropriate texts meeting these aspects:

> "Who his own self bare our sins in his own body on the tree." "Whom God set forth to be a propitiation through faith in his blood, to declare his righteousness for the remission of sins that are past, through the forbearance of God." "The blood of Jesus Christ his Son cleanses us from all sin." "Except a man be born from above, he cannot see the kingdom of God." "If any man be in Christ, he is a new creation. Old things are passed away; behold all things have

become new." "The law of the Spirit of life in Christ Jesus hath made us free from the law of sin and death." "Stand fast, therefore, in the liberty wherewith Christ hath made you free, and be not entangled again in the yoke of bondage." "For this purpose the Son of God was manifested, that he might destroy the works of the devil." "To declare, I say, his righteousness, that he might be just, and the justifier of him that believeth in Jesus."

Pierson used the KJV, which was quite satisfactory for his purpose, but in one instance more recent versions correct a KJV rendering. See Romans 3:25 (RSV), which correctly has "he had passed over former sins." The meaning is NOT that justification only cancels the sins of the believer's past, but rather that God had not exacted full penalty for sin before the Cross. We continue now quoting from Pierson's lecture:

> First of all, there must be a legal satisfaction to broken law. … The broken law of God must be honoured and maintained; the death penalty must be executed. … Secondly, such satisfaction is provided by substitution. … Redemption is not only by satisfaction to a broken law, and by substitution of the innocent for the guilty, but it is on the principle of representation which is a step in advance even on substitution (Ex. 28:36-43).

> This redemption is inseparable from regeneration. The Holy Spirit of God supplements and complements the atoning work of Jesus Christ on the Cross—Christ expiating penalty, and cleansing guilt; the Holy Spirit, changing the very nature, and so implanting the germ of a holy character. Not only an imputed righteousness, but an imparted righteousness, belongs to the scheme of redemption. …

> The scheme of salvation, which starts with satisfaction and proceeds to substitution, then to representation, and then to regeneration, ends and is consummated with eternal identification with the Redeemer.

> The question naturally arises whether the moral ends of punishment are met and satisfied in such vicarious atonement. We need to ask, therefore, another preliminary question as to what the moral ends of punishment are; and all will agree that they are somewhat as follows:

1. Law, as a broken code, must be honoured and magnified by due infliction of penalty.

2. Guilt, as guilt, must be exhibited in its enormity and deformity.

3. The sanctions of government must be so upheld that none may sin with impunity.

4. So far as possible, forgiven offenders must be reclaimed and reformed.

5. Other offenders must be deterred from similar offences.

6. God himself must be vindicated as an absolutely holy God.

Pierson then elaborates how Calvary met all these moral ends. See his book *God's Living Oracles*, chapters eight and nine.

It is important to understand that Christ's atonement includes his life of obedience and suffering as well as his last hours. A. A. Hodge wrote:

> The whole earth life of Christ, including His birth itself, was one continued self-emptying, even unto death. His birth, and every moment of his life, in the form of a servant, was of the nature of holy sufferings. Every experience of pain during the whole course of his life, and eminently in His death on the cross, was, on his part, a voluntary and meritorious act of obedience. He lived His whole life, from His birth to His death, as our Representative, obeying and suffering in our stead, and for our sakes, and during this whole course, all His suffering was obedience, and all His obedience was suffering. … His earth life as suffering cancels the penalty, and as obedience, fulfils the precepts and secures the promised reward of the law.…"
>
> Cited by Arthur Pink, *The Atonement*, p. 64

As W. Shedd pointed out, "Christ's circumcision was as really a part of His vicarious atonement, as the blood that flowed from His pierced side." And Pink also quotes W. Syminton, "Not one throb of pain did He feel, not one pang of sorrow did He experience, not one sigh of anguish did He heave, not one tear of grief did He shed, for Himself. All were for men, all were for us" (*Ibid.*, pp. 88,73).

The Old Testament is full of types and symbols pointing to the Atonement. Consider the first seven significant references to blood as found in Genesis and Exodus:

The blood cries	Genesis 4:10
The blood is sacred	Genesis 9:4
The blood presented to the Father	Genesis 37:31,32
The blood demands a reckoning	Genesis 42:22
The blood cleanses	Genesis 49:11
The blood is a sign of judgment	Exodus 4:9
Only the blood protects and preserves	Exodus 12:13

Consider also the key references to the Lamb:

The lamb typified	Genesis 3:21
The lamb prophesied	Genesis 22:1-14
The lamb's blood applied	Exodus 12:13
The lamb personified	Isaiah 53
The lamb identified	John 1:29;
The lamb magnified	Revelation 5:6-14
The lamb glorified	Revelation 22:1

The feasts of Israel were all typical, and the Passover, the Day of Atonement, and the ushering in of the Jubilee particularly pointed to the redemption to be accomplished at the Cross. At the Passover, only those who had applied the blood were safe. On the Day of Atonement the High Priest officiated in the garments of a common priest, and only he did all the work of that day, and for the first time in the year he entered the Most Holy Place with sacrificial blood to sprinkle over the broken Law. When the Atonement was complete, he left his garments in the sanctuary (as Christ left his grave clothes in the tomb) and emerged from the holy places to unite with a joyous community, which then accompanied him to his home. The Jubilee began every fiftieth year when the Day of Atonement was completed, and it announced the dissolution of all debts and slavery, and made possible restoration to forfeited inheritances.

The tiny book of Ruth is a miniature Bible with its story of the redemption of an alien exiled by law, but admitted by grace, through the goodness of a kinsman-redeemer. Synonyms for "redeemer" occur 30 times in that little book. In the fourth chapter the word "redemption" in found five times in one verse, nine times in three verses. In the tenth verse Boaz announces that he has purchased Ruth to be his wife by redeeming the alienated property. Pierson says, "Nothing can explain the extreme minuteness of detail here except a typical design on the part of the inspiring Spirit" (*God's Living Oracles*, p. 156).

Ada R. Habershon in *The Study of the Types*, p. 45, lists the types of Calvary she recognizes:

1. Where there was actual shedding of blood

The coats of skins	A covering
Abel's sacrifice	Acceptance
Gen. 22, "*Jehovah Jireh*"	Substitution provided
The paschal lamb	Deliverance from wrath
The burnt-offering	Acceptance
The peace-offering	Peace and fellowship
The sin and trespass offering	Forgiveness
The Day of Atonement	Atonement
The red heifer	Cleansing
The bird in Leviticus 14	Cleansing and justification
The suckling lamb	Christ crucified in weakness, our strength
The one found slain	His death required

2. Christ passing through the waters of death

Jonah	The time in the grave
The ark	The only means of safety
The Red Sea	Deliverance from our enemies
The Jordan	Entrance into blessing
Stones in the Jordan	Union in death and resurrection and the land
The tree cast into *Marah*	Bitter turned into sweet
The branch into Jordan	Uplifting that which is sunken

3. Other types

The smitten rock	The gift of the Spirit because of Calvary
The brazen serpent	The healing from the bite of sin
Adam's sleep	The building up of the church
The rent veil	Access to God
The corn of wheat	The source of the harvest

Now we append some comments from some who devoted far more time to the Old Testament pictures of Christ than most of us have to the New Testament ones. I wish I could claim authorship of the immediately following lines but I cannot. I do not know the authors of the first two paragraphs.

> Suffering and sin and love are the ABC of the world's long night, the theme of all great literature, the subject of all great painting, the key to all great music. This is the eternal triangle and at its apex stands the Cross. There he suffered as none has ever suffered. He bore sin as none other ever could. He loved as none other ever would.

> The paradox of the Passion: "the mighty weakness of the dying Christ. Never was suffering more triumphant, silence more eloquent, love more powerful, meekness so mighty. Never was submission so plainly the way to mastery, truth rejected so unanswerable, exhaustion so near omnipotence."

> Remember that it is the innocent moon, that nothing does but shine, that moves all the labouring surges of the world.[3]

J. H. Newman, well-known cleric of the nineteenth century wrote:

> The Christ of the Cross and the Cross of Christ constitute the key to the world and to life. At Calvary, we find our great lesson, how to think of and how to deal with this world.

> The Cross alone puts a true estimate upon everything we see or experience—all that seems good or evil, all "advantages," all "promotions" or "demotions," all pleasures, excitements, rivalries, hopes, fears, desires, efforts, and "triumphs" of mortal man. It gives a meaning to the various shifting experiences of life—its trials, temptations, and sufferings. It brings together and makes consistent all that seems discordant and aimless.

> The Cross teaches us how to live, how to use this world, what to expect, desire, hope. It is the tone into which all the strains of this world's music are ultimately to be resolved.

---

[3]   This fragment is taken from a poem by Francis Thompson "Part the Second," in *Sister Songs an Offering to Two Sisters,* Charleston, BiblioBazaar LLC, 2009, p. 36.

It is a superficial view to say that life is made chiefly for pleasure. To those who look under the surface it tells a different tale. The Cross teaches the very same lesson which this world teaches to those who live long in it, who have much experience in it, who discern its real nature. The surface of the world is bright, but the Cross is both sorrowful and glorious. Truth is not on the surface of things but in the depths.

Let us not trust the world nor give our hearts to it. Let us not begin with it. Rather let us begin with faith. Let us begin with Christ. They alone are truly able to enjoy this world who begin with the world unseen. They alone can truly feast who have first fasted. They alone can use the world who have learned not to abuse it. They alone inherit this world who take it as a shadow of the world to come and who, for that world to come, relinquish it.

And now from a contemporary of Newman but on the opposite continent, a woman with little education apart from her wide reading:

Under and around the Cross, that immortal pillar, sin shall never revive, nor error obtain control. In the Cross all influence centers and from it all influence goes forth. It is the great Center of attraction. Hanging upon the Cross, Christ was the gospel. This is our message, our argument, our doctrine, our warning to the impenitent, our encouragement for the sorrowing, the hope for every believer. By the Cross the law and the gospel are presented as a perfect whole. Only here were God's holiness and love equally displayed. To remove the Cross from the Christian would be like blotting the sun from the sky. Ellen G. White, *Letter 24,* 1900

Man could not atone for man—his sinful imperfect condition would constitute him an imperfect offering. Christ was priest and victim. Had God pardoned Adam's sin without an atonement, sin would have been immortalized. The gulf between heaven and earth was bridged by the Cross. At an infinite cost Christ purchased the human race. The Cross was Christ's victory and the victory of all who believe in him. In comparison with the knowledge of God revealed by the Cross all other knowledge is as chaff. Christ's Cross drew mercy and justice across the separating gulf sin had made. Ellen G. White, *Lift Him Up,* p. 16

And now a French writer:

> In the light of the Cross, how could there be any doubt about the three propositions at the heart of the Christian position? The sheer and utter evilness of evil is demonstrated there. ... The complete sovereignty of God is demonstrated there. ... All this happened "by God's set purpose and foreknowledge" (Acts 2:23). ... The unadulterated goodness of God is demonstrated there. At the Cross, who would dare entertain the blasphemy of imagining that God would even to the slightest degree, comply with evil? It brought him death, in the person of his Son. Holiness stands revealed. Love stands revealed, a pure love, there is no love greater. Because of the Cross we shall praise his goodness, the goodness of his justice, the goodness of his grace, through all eternity. At the Cross, God turned evil against evil and brought about the practical solution to the problem. He has made atonement for sin, he has conquered death, he has triumphed over the devil. ... What further demonstration do we need?

Henri Blocher, *Evil and the Cross*, p. 104

Chapter 13

The Forensic Theory of Justification

The Richard Hammill Memorial Lecture, Campus Hill Church, Loma Linda, California, September 6, 2008. Speaker: Desmond Ford.

I am very glad to be here. At my age I am glad to be anywhere.

I beg of you, don't be put off by the title assigned me for this talk. It could just have easily been, "What is the chief metaphor in the Bible for how to be right with God right now, regardless of sinfulness, weakness, and failures?"

Usually in a talk of this nature technicalities prevail but I have put the necessary ones in the paper we have given you. I wish to be very practical—Most of you I will never meet again, and I am responsible to God for what I say in this hour.

A little girl who asked too many questions was told that curiosity killed the cat. "What did the cat want to know?" asked the young lady.

What do you want to know? This meditation is about what we should want to know. Life is a triangle. We have a relationship with ourselves, with others and with God. But until I know that God accepts me I cannot accept myself. And if I cannot accept myself I will never accept others. Being right with God is the chief business of life. Well, here's how. Justification answers our chief question.

The Bible says the unrighteous will not enter the kingdom of heaven, but it also says that there are none righteous. So that's a problem.

Trying to earn righteousness is like spitting into the ocean to raise its level, or its like eating soup with a fork. It's like trying to get water uphill with a rake. You get nowhere.

The solution to this conundrum the Bible calls justification—the NIV translates that term on occasion as "declared righteous."

The Greek term for justification is a forensic one—that means a legal one—associated with law, judges, courts, but particularly law. Scholars universally agree on this and anyone with a concordance can quickly prove it. The Greek *dik* family (righteousness) in the New Testament is the equivalent of the *sadaq* family in the Old Testament. It also means "righteousness," and in the Hiphil form it carries the meaning of "declare righteous." Davidson's *Hebrew Grammar* gives several examples on page 95. There are about 500 *sadaq* terms in the Old Testament, and over 40 are verbs. In the New Testament Greek equivalent there are over 200 instances and again the verb means "to declare righteous." Please note that the forerunner of the New Testament term comes from the Hebrew Old Testament and not secular Greek.

Forensic is not a negative or a bad word. It offers the key to the universe, for it is saying that things are not haphazard. Law is not God's creation, it is God's nature. The secret of abounding lasting joy is harmony with law—physical law, mental law, spiritual law. Where there is no law, relationships between people become chaotic and deadly.

To be legal and to be legalistic are two different things as being rational and rationalistic are. Your marriage, I trust, is legal, but hopefully not legalistic.

So law was intended for our well-being, our enduring happiness. But something has thrown a spanner in the works. That something is sin—hatred of God and excessive love of self—selfishness. Christ took this reality for granted. He once said, "If ye then being evil…." He also said that unless we loved him more than our own life we would be eternally lost. Sometime read the last verses of Mark 9, but not before having your supper.

> What then shall we say to the great Judge in whose sight the heavens are not clean, who charges his angels with folly, by whose strength the mountains are melted, by whose brightness the sky is darkened, by whose anger the earth is shaken? Who among us shall dwell "with the devouring fire? Who among us shall dwell with everlasting burnings?" (Isa. 33:14). "He that has clean hands and a pure heart." The one whose obedience to God is flawless in heart and hand and walk, willing, (for unwilling obedience is like a sacrifice without fire), complete (for he that keeps the whole law yet ails in one point is guilt of all—James 2:10), consistent (from childhood till death).

Remember the Scripture says our iniquities are more than the hairs of our head and that the very best of persons are only vanity. Which of us can ask, "Who convicts me of sin?" Which of us has fulfilled the law "Be ye therefore perfect"?
(Bill Gravestock)

Because of our prevailing failures the Law is now against us. Sin is lawlessness and the wages of sin is death. Because the problem has to do with law, so must the solution. The solution has to be forensic because we are judgment bound.

Please understand this. Justification is a metaphor for the forgiveness of sins. It is more than that—it is acquittal, and more than that it is imputation of the righteousness of Christ.

But the basis of justification in the believer's experience is the forgiveness of sins—that is the door into the temple beautiful of the Christian life. This is what Christianity is about.

"Where sin abounds, grace does much more abound." "By grace are you saved through faith, and that not of yourselves, it is the gift of God." Paul's epistles begin and end with grace. Grace is God's undeserved overflowing mercy for the worst of men and women freely offered to all, however far gone they are. Because of grace, righteousness in the New Testament is called a gift. That is how it is described six times in Romans five. God is in the business of offering undeserved mercy to the selfish, the greedy, the impure, the hateful, the avaricious, the apathetic, the lazy, the liar, the self-righteous, the adulterer and the murderer. Read Luke 6:35, which says God is kind to the ungrateful and to the evil. What a verse! What a truth! What a God!

Only God is given away, only heaven can be had for the asking. Barabbas was a killer, but Christ took his place. The penitent thief had all his life been a rogue, but Christ offered him Paradise. The woman caught in adultery was ready to be stoned, but Christ said, "Neither do I condemn thee—go and sin no more." How could he say that? It was because he was about to pay the price of her sin.

All our sins are a grain of sand alongside the mountain of God's grace, a spark dropping into the ocean of his mercy. God is more willing to forgive than a mother to pluck her child from a burning building. It would be easier to take the blaze from the sun, or the salt from the sea than to take mercy from the heart of God.

You don't have to be good to be saved. You have to be saved to be good. You come to him just as you are, but he never leaves you just as you are. It's not really a matter of who you are, but whose you are. "This man receives sinners." Are you one? He will receive you. "He has gone to be guest with him that is a sinner." Do you want him as your guest?

Our part is to accept his gift—faith. That's why we read of justification BY FAITH. The best things can't just be given without a response. They have to be accepted. You may want to give your child an education, but much of it is up to him or her. And it is up to us to respond to the moving of the Spirit and to extend the beggar's hand to receive the gift. Faith also is God's gift as we hear the gospel, provided we do not reject the message. We are not saved because of faith but through faith. It's not meritorious. Accepting the gift breaks our heart and the tide of love and gratitude always leads to obedience. True faith is a busy active thing and works through love. God gives his gifts with both hands. Justification and sanctification are distinct but never separate.

You have heard of the philosopher Bertrand Russell. He was a great mover and shaker, and a womanizer, but no Christian. He wrote a book entitled *Why I Am Not a Christian.*

His daughter said about her parents—speaking of the religion in which they had been raised. "They had a religion of dry morality without grace. Its demands were many and impossible. Consequently they were defeated and depressed."

So it has been with multitudes of Seventh-day Adventists. In 1888 when justification by faith was preached at Minneapolis Ellen White said, "This is the first teaching on this subject I have heard from human lips in forty-five years except in conversations with my husband." What were we doing in those forty-five years? We were preaching the law until we were "as dry as the hills of Gilboa." Paul said that he died to the law that he might live unto God. See Galatians 2:19. We are to die to law as a method but never as a standard.

There is a beautiful statement in *Steps to Christ*:

> There are those who profess to serve God, while they rely upon their own efforts to obey his law, to form a right character, and secure salvation. Their hearts are not moved by any deep sense of the love of Christ. But they seek to perform the duties of the Christian life

as that which God requires of them in order to gain heaven. Such religion is worth nothing … and is heavy drudgery."
(Chapter "Consecration")

So there are two groups in every church—those who serve him lovingly and those who serve him legalistically. Adventism will never take the gospel to the world until it understands justification. See the story of the Pharisee and the woman who anointed Christ's feet in Luke chapter seven. As long as we think we have been forgiven little, we love little and serve little. If you now are serving little, it is because you don't know God and you don't know the gospel.

No one ever loves God until convinced God loves him or her. And remember the first and great commandment is to love God. It is impossible without the gospel, and the gospel is best expressed in the forensic truth of justification. As you can't hammer a rosebud open, neither can you force a person to believe in the love of God. God loves us into loving him.

Justification is the opposite of condemnation. See Romans chapters five and eight. It does not mean to make righteous. "The Christian is always a sinner, always a penitent, and always right with God." You will always need to pray the Lord's Prayer, "forgive us…." According to James 3:2, "in many things we all offend." But despite sinfulness we are accepted in the beloved and complete in him, and we stand without condemnation. Our failures are not recorded against us. See Romans 4:8.

Second Corinthians 5:14-21 and the story of Gethsemane and Calvary explain how these things can be. These verses overthrow and demolish the moral influence theory, which denies that Christ's death was a sacrifice. Read Mark 14:33-34. Christ almost died in Gethsemane. It was as though he had seen a terrible apparition and received a dreadful shock, which chilled his blood and paralysed his nerves. The burden of the world's guilt was placed upon him and the second death began. "He was made to be sin for us that we might be made the righteousness of God in him."

This explains the awful cry from the Cross, "My God, My God, Why…?" He really was forsaken. God could not smile upon the prisoner at the bar. He represented the whole rebellious world. And it was the withdrawing of the Father's presence in consequence, not the crucifixion, which killed Christ. The blackness over the sun signified the absence of light in the mind and heart of our Redeemer. "Hope did not present to him his coming forth from the grave as a conqueror."

Study Romans 5:10,18. "When we were God's enemies we were reconciled to him through the death of his Son...." "Just as the result of one trespass was condemnation for all men, so also the result of one act of righteousness was justification that brings life for all men." We were ruined without asking for it—by a representative. And we were saved without asking for it—by a Representative. Now can say with Luther, "Mine are Christ's living and dying as though I had lived his life and died his death." We were crucified with Christ, buried with Christ, we rose with Christ, and now we are seated in the heavenly places with Christ. See Galatians 2:20; Romans 6:4; Colossians 3:1; and Ephesians 2:6. Surely this is the good, glad and merry tidings which make the heart to sing, and the feet to dance. Here is the one subject that should swallow up every other—the one thing needful, the sweetest melody of human lips.

This is the message that converted Augustine, Luther, Wesley, Spurgeon, and millions through them. When God uses a truth to change the lives of multitudes we must be very careful how we deal with it. It is blasphemy to repudiate the obvious work of the Holy Spirit. Christ promised that his Spirit would lead the church into truth, and the supreme truth of the ages is this—that God justifies the ungodly. See Romans 4:5. This is the most amazing fact in the universe.

There are about 10 metaphors for salvation, but justification is the chief one. It is referred to about 70 times in Paul's Epistles, whereas propitiation as a synonym for the Cross occurs only four times and reconciliation five, and ransom three. Justification is not mentioned in every Epistle but it is taken for granted in all. When referred to briefly it is not explained for his readers knew all about it. The earliest reference was probably Galatians 1:6-9. Read it and read it again.

> I am astonished that you are so quickly deserting the one who called you by the grace of Christ and are turning to a different gospel—which is really no gospel at all ... even if we or an angel from heaven should preach a gospel other than the one we preached to you, let him be eternally condemned....

The gospel is not like plasticine. It is changeless like God. It is everlasting. It has power. Study Romans 1:16-17 in many translations. Read the word "power"—*dunamis*. Paul was not tolerant regarding the gospel and neither should we be (Acts 4:12).

Christ made the atonement but Paul explained it. In his first and longest Epistle he set forth justification in the first five chapters. This is the most important document in all history except for the Gospels. It has changed the lives of millions. F. F. Bruce said it is inviting cataclysmic change to study Romans, but a change so much for the better.

Paul wrote letters to seven churches. The last letter is to the Thessalonians and it is about the Second Advent. But the first letter is about the gospel. None of us are ready for the Second Advent until we know the gospel. This is where Adventism corporately has failed.

Looking briefly at Romans, we find it is written like a lawyer's brief. The first chapter tell us that unbelievers are lost, and the second chapter says that even a profession of faith is insufficient to save. In chapter three we are told that the whole world is condemned and lost. There is a dramatic pause for three days and then a Mediator arises saying "But now," and verses 21 to 28 of chapter three set forth the essence of justification by faith.

Read the *Living Bible* paraphrase of Romans 3:19ff.:

> Now do you see it? No one can ever be made right in God's sight by doing what the law commands. For the more we know of God's laws the clearer it becomes that we aren't obeying them; his laws serve only to make us see that we are sinners.

> But now God has shown us a different way to heaven—not by being "good enough" and trying to keep his laws, but by a new way (though not new really, for the Scriptures told about it long ago). Now God says he will accept and acquit us—declare us "not guilty"—if we trust Jesus Christ to take away our sins. And we can all be saved in this same way, by coming to Christ, no matter who we are, or what we have been.

In the first chapters we are told that through the gospel we are free from the wrath of God (chapters one to three), free from guilt (chapter four), free from condemnation (chapter five), free from the dominion of sin (chapter six), free from the law as a method (chapter seven), and free from death (chapter eight). What good news indeed!

Some of my friends will say to me, "Des, what about the New Perspective on Paul"? It means nothing to most of you though it has caused a sea change in theology in the last 40 years. But remember, "if it's old it may not be pure gold; and if it's new, its rarely true." The one who marries the Spirit of the age quickly becomes a widower. Let me point out that the theory chiefly exists in English-speaking countries—this theory that we have been wrong about Paul and justification. Many top scholars ignore it, or academically demolish it. In recent years its key areas have come under very heavy, but legitimate criticism.

Listen, if you, like me, are aware of being very imperfect, justification is for you. To understand justification as the Bible's chief metaphor for the forgiveness of sins, which is the primary biblical doctrine—this is what brings heaven very near. Heaven is not light years away—it is yours now if you believe that God loves you as though there was no one else to love.

Two men who carried heaven with them everywhere they went preached and sang the gospel as no one had done for over a century. They were the Wesley brothers. Here is why they were so happy and spread joy to so many. I give you the words of Charles Wesley, the world's greatest hymn-writer:

> And can it be, that I should gain
> An interest in my Saviour's blood?
> Died he for me who caused him pain,
> For me who him to death pursued?
> Amazing love, how can it be,
> That thou my God should die for me?
>
> No condemnation now I dread
> Jesus and all in him are mine,
> Alive in him my living head,
> And clothed in righteousness divine,
> Bold I approach the eternal throne
> And claim the crown, through Christ, my own.

If this is the gospel on which you stake your faith. If this is the essence of your personal faith, will you stand with me and witness for the gospel and for Christ this very evening?

(Hundreds stand and come to the front.)

Benediction.

Chapter 14

Men and Women Who Knew The True Gospel and Changed the World

Paul of Tarsus, next to Christ, is the most important man who ever lived. He changed the world drastically, and even today all of us are surrounded by influences that stem from him.

Sir William Mitchell Ramsay, one of the most brilliant scholars of classical learning wrote:

> Of all the men of the first century, incomparably the most influential was the Apostle Paul. No one man exercised anything like so much power as he did in moulding the future of the Empire.… Had it not been for Paul … no man would now remember Greek and Roman civilization.
>
> Barbarism proved too powerful for the Graeco-Roman civilization unaided by the new religious bond; and every channel through which that civilization was preserved, or interest in it maintained, either is now or has been in some essential part of its course Christian after the Pauline form.
>
> *Pauline and Other Studies*, pp. 53, 100, cited by Wilbur M. Smith, *Therefore Stand*, pp. 246-247

Adolphe Monod, in his French lectures, gave the following opinion:

> Should any one ask me to name the man of whom all others has been the greatest benefactor of the race, I should say without hesitation the Apostle Paul. His name is the type of human activity the most

endless, and at the same time the most useful, that history has cared to preserve.

Cited by H.T. Kuist, *The Pedagogy of St Paul*, p. 136

New Testament scholar James Stalker says, "We owe to him hundreds of ideas which were never uttered before" (*The Life of St. Paul*, p. 93).

Historian Kuist tells us that it was the result of Paul's extensive teaching travels throughout the known world, that turned a Jewish sect into a world religion. Thus the Occident and the Orient were united, and the history of Europe predetermined.

One half of the most influential book in the world, the New Testament, owes its origin to Paul. He himself wrote a quarter of it, and his friend Luke wrote another quarter providing the only information about the apostle that we have outside of the Epistles. Furthermore, more books have been written about this man and his ideas that about any other character in history, Jesus Christ excepted. He was the spark that kindled many later minds of genius who subsequently influenced Western culture.

In the year 396 A.D., Augustine, with troubled mind and heart, was walking in a garden near Milan when he heard the voice of a child singing, "Take, read!" Near him was a copy of Paul's *Letter to the Romans*. On opening this, Augustine's eye fell on a passage so appropriate to his present condition and mood that his whole life was thereupon changed. Millions today believe that the new Augustine (despite his many errors) became an incalculable blessing to the whole Christian world.

In a monastery cell centuries later, a miner's son turned priest read the same letter of Paul's. This transformed and energized him. Martin Luther became a leader in an age longing for a revival of religion and morality.

John Wesley, the man who saved England from a bloody revolution similar to that in France, the founder of Methodism, and author of over two hundred books, found his way to an unparalleled life of service as a result of insight gained into one of Paul's major concepts—Justification by Faith.

In the field of oratory Paul has been similarly influential. Here are a few of those who have been motivated by this ancient Jew. Chrysostom, Origen, Ambrose, Augustine, Bernard, Wycliffe, Latimer, Knox, Luther, Calvin,

Bossuet, Bourdaloue, Fenelon, Baxter, Wesley, Spurgeon, Beecher, Brooks, Talmage, Fulton Sheen, and Billy Graham. Secular speakers also should be listed, such as Wilberforce, Bright, and William Jennings Bryan.

C.E. Jefferson offers an impressive summary:

> When he speaks to us, mysterious powers awaken in us. He quickens us, kindles us, arouses us to aspire and dream. We have to reckon with him as a world force. He is a potent factor in social evolution. He is one of the determining influences in our Western civilization. The prints of his fingers are on our institutions. His ethical ideals stand in the marketplace. His ideas are running in our blood. He has woven himself into the fibre of our consciences and conduct. We are influenced by him even when we are least conscious of him … the whole world would today be different had Saul of Tarsus never lived.

The Character of Paul, p. 375

Originally a bigoted, intolerant, and fierce persecutor, this Pharisee of the Pharisees saw the risen Christ and received a commission from him such as no other person has ever received. If he was deluded in this, we must attribute to coincidence the strange conformity of his later history and achievements to the message he believed Christ gave him that day. It is hardly sufficient to say that Luke invented the story, for most fabricators would have been far more careful to make the three accounts apparently harmonious in every detail. It is the very carelessness of the chronicler in this regard that suggests the honesty of his narration. Certainly the phenomenon of the Epistles, and Paul's unique global influence, requires a cause, which, if not identical with that given in Acts, must yet be as miraculous.

In Philippians chapter three Paul tells of his conversion. It was his learning from Christ that righteousness was a divine gift, and that the righteousness of the law, however flawlessly obeyed, could never meet heaven's standard—this turned Paul's world upside down, and made him the greatest of the Apostles. And millions who have learned the difference between the righteousness which is of faith and the righteousness of the Law have given a similar testimony.

Martin Luther (1483-1546)

In the sixteenth century it must have seemed that the religion of the day was a far cry from the simple faith of the churches addressed in the New Testament. Rare copies of the Bible were chained to monastery walls, more effectually sealed by the unknown sacred languages of the Old and New Testaments than by any outward inhibiting barriers to possession or understanding. Historian Roland Bainton sketches other problems confronting the Christian faith:

> The popes of the Renaissance were secularized, flippant, frivolous, sensual, magnificent, and unscrupulous. The intelligentsia did not revolt against the Church because the Church was so much of their mind and mood as scarcely to warrant a revolt. Politics were emancipated from any concern for the faith to such a degree that the Most Christian King of France and His Holiness the Pope did not disdain a military alliance with the Sultan against the Holy Roman Empire.
>
> *Here I Stand*, pp. 15

Let it not be thought that religion was *in absentia*. It was quite the contrary. Religion permeated every aspect of life. On every hand could be seen steeples and spires, monasteries and priests, and religious processions and shrines. Mediaeval theology induced tensions which were far removed from the "righteousness, peace, and joy" (Romans 14:17) of the apostolic faith, but the failure was not from the lack of trying to be good. The prevailing fashion in mediaeval piety was to provoke alternately fear and hope. Again we refer to Bainton:

> Hell was stoked, not because men lived in perpetual dread, but precisely because they did not, and in order to instil enough fear to drive them to the sacraments of the Church. If they were petrified with terror, purgatory was introduced by way of mitigation as an intermediate place where those not bad enough for hell, nor good enough for heaven, might make further expiation. If the alleviation inspired complacency, the temperature was advanced on purgatory, and then the pressure was again relaxed through indulgences.
>
> *Ibid.*, p. 20-21

Catholic man is no worse nor better than Protestant man, and vice versa, for we are confronted with a return to similar degeneration of faith and practice in the Protestantism of two centuries later.

It was a fierce thunderstorm in the year 1505 A.D., which precipitated a young university student to his knees and elicited his promise to become a monk. But he found no peace in the monastery. Confessions, sometimes six hours in length, did little for him. But one day the Spirit of God gave him the most important insight in the world—that the righteousness required by God was his gift to the empty hand of the penitent sinner. He wrote concerning this:

> I greatly longed to understand Paul's Epistle to the Romans and nothing stood in the way but that one expression, "the righteousness of God," because I took it to mean that righteousness whereby God is just and deals justly in punishing the unrighteous. My situation was that, although an impeccable monk, I stood before God as a sinner troubled in conscience, and I had no confidence that my merit would assuage him. Therefore I did not love a just and angry God, but rather hated and murmured against him. Yet I clung to the dear Paul and had a great yearning to know what he meant.
>
> Night and day I pondered until I saw the connection between "the righteousness of God" and the statement that "the just shall live by his faith." Then I grasped that the righteousness of God is that righteousness by which through grace and sheer mercy God justifies us through faith. Thereupon I felt myself to be reborn and to have gone through open doors into Paradise. The whole of Scripture took on a new meaning, and whereas before the "righteousness of God" had filled me with hate, now it became to me inexpressibly sweet in greater love. This passage of Paul became to me a gate to heaven.
>
> If you have a true faith that Christ is your Saviour, then at once you have a gracious God, for faith leads you in and opens up God's heart and will, that you should see pure grace and overflowing love. This it is to behold God in faith that you should look upon his fatherly, friendly heart, in which there is no anger nor ungraciousness. He who sees God as angry does not see him rightly but looks only on a curtain, as if a dark cloud had been drawn across his face.

Ibid., p. 50 (Mentor edition)

In other words, as J. S. Whale has put it, "Romans 1:16-17 is not a judge's merciless verdict against us, but a Father's costly gift to us."

To Luther, justification by faith alone was central, fundamental, and final. But this meant the rejection of centuries of religious teaching. The Church of Rome did not consider Christ's redemptive work as the only ground of salvation. It chose to supplement it by human merit. Whale's splendid book *The Protestant Tradition*, shows the manner in which Rome neutralized all that Augustine had said about grace. It did this by the semi-pelagianism (dependence on human effort) of its sacerdotal system whereby sacramental grace and meritorious human works were ever at the fore.

Luther had been taught that righteousness was infused into those who partook of the sacraments, especially the Mass, baptism, and penance. A newborn baby had to be baptized immediately, lest death overtook it, with resultant everlasting hell-fire. Because of this terrible teaching a special medical instrument was invented to make intrauterine baptism possible for a baby dying inside the womb.

The obedient Catholic understood that while salvation was possible because of grace, only human merit could make it actual. And even if everything was done as the church prescribed, there was no certainty of salvation. Assurance regarding one's relationship with God was considered presumptuous. But Luther, Wesley, Whitefield, and Spurgeon all recognized that in the New Testament assurance was not only every Christian's privilege, but also their happy duty. It is indeed the glory of true Protestantism.

Luther has often been criticized for his very severe verbal castigations of the Jews, but it should be remembered that no man had laboured as hard as he to convert them, and furthermore, he never advocated physical violence against them. Recognizing that all the saints are fallible, let us rejoice in this fact that God used Luther to restore that gospel which had been buried for centuries.

Laeuchi's classic, *The Language of Faith*, has documented the early loss of the Pauline gospel. With Tertullian in the second century, nomism replaced saving faith. Cyprian in the third century transmitted this to what became the mediaeval church. Thus within two generations the New Testament emphases on grace and faith alone were submerged by legalism which is the oldest of religious heresies.

Another classic, Koberle's, *The Quest for Holiness*, has this to say:

The church did not guard the message of justification as carefully as she should have. The momentous dissolution and disintegration of that truth began very early, and has continued to the present day, as human activities and demonstrable experiences are mingled with the gospel of the forgiveness of sins. Instead of the final, complete promise of God, that requires no supplementing, there is again substituted a gradual transformation reached by a habitual infusion of righteousness. Whether this infusion be of a sacramental, mystical, or spiritualistic sort, in every case, in the place of God's pardoning word, which establishes a new relationship, there is substituted a dynamic process by which our certainty of the possession of an unshakable basis of justification is again lost.

> p. 58 ff.

Norval Pease, in his *By Faith Alone*, page 81, put it more simply: "As the struggle with Judaism abated, the simpler and more natural philosophy of salvation through obedience became more and more prominent."

And James Orr writes similarly:

There is no question, then, from the Protestant, and I believe also from the Scriptural standpoint, but that the Church, from a very early period, went seriously astray in its doctrinal and practical apprehension of the divine method of the sinner's salvation. ... In train of this, as its natural consequence, came the use of the term "justification" to cover the entire change supposed to be effected in baptism—both the divine forgiveness and the divine renewal; in other words, the taking of justification to mean, not as in Pauline usage, the absolving of a sinner from guilt, and declaring him to be righteous in God's sight, but peculiarly the making of the sinner righteous by infusing into him a new nature, then, ... declaring him righteous. ... post-baptismal sins, as not covered by the initial justification, had to be expiated in some other way, by good works and satisfactions of the sinner's own. On the ground thus laid down was built in due course the whole elaborate system of penance in the Romish Church.

The Progress of Dogma, p. 247 ff.

And to quote yet another classic, this time by Mackintosh, *The Christian Experience of Forgiveness* p. 113 ff.:

> In the patristic age, the great New Testament idea of justification by faith, although not denied outright, was very imperfectly understood. It can hardly be said to have been understood at all.

A more recent writer, Edward J. Carnell tells us:

> Roman Catholicism merges justification and sanctification, but this does not have the hallmark of Scripture. Justification is declaratory; sanctification is constitutive. Justification takes place once; sanctification is a lifelong process. Justification is a change in the sinner's relation to God; sanctification is a change in the sinner himself. Justification is objective; sanctification is subjective. Justification is an act done for us; sanctification is an act done in us.

> *The Case for Orthodox Theology*, pp. 73-74

We offer one more example of the faith that came to possess Luther and which became the basis of the Protestant Reformation. This quotation should be studied and read repeatedly.

> Sin is self-assertion, disobedience, and rebellion; and in regard to Adam's true relation to God there were three results of his sin:

> a.   A sense of guilt (Gen. 3:8); (b) A sentence of condemnation (Gen. 3:16-19); (c) An act of separation (Gen. 3:23). Thus the true relation to God was forfeited, and these results abide today, and apply to all mankind apart from God.

> Now justification is connected with the restoration of this true relation to God. It includes (a) The removal of Condemnation by the bestowal of Forgiveness; (b) the removal of Guilt by the reckoning (or imputation) of Righteousness; (c) the removal of Separation by the restoration of Fellowship.

> Justification, then, means the re-instatement of man in his original relation to God. It means to treat him as righteous in the sight of God, to account him righteous, to regard him as righteous, to declare

him righteous. It means that man is accepted as righteous in the eyes of the law, and restored to a true position before God.

Justification is, therefore, much more than pardon, and the two must never be confused, much less identified. Forgiveness is only a part of justification, and to identify them is to cause spiritual trouble and loss. We can see the two distinguished in Acts 13:38-39 and in Psalm 32:1-2. A criminal may be pardoned, but he cannot be regarded as though he had never broken the law. Forgiveness is only negative, the removal of the condemnation. Justification is also positive, the removal of guilt, and the bestowal of a perfect standing before God. Forgiveness is an act, and a succession of acts from time to time. Justification is an act, which results in a permanent attitude or position in the sight of God.

Forgiveness is repeated throughout our life. Justification is complete and never repeated, and since it refers to our spiritual position before God, it covers the whole of our life, past, present, and future. We can see the distinction in our Lord's words, "He that has been bathed (justification) needs not save to wash his feet (forgiveness)" (John 13:10). He that has once had the bath of a perfect justification needs only the daily cleansing of the soul through forgiveness, not a fresh justification.

Justification is also different from making righteous, which, as we shall see hereafter, is sanctification. The two are always inseparable in reality, but they are assuredly distinguishable in thought, and must always be distinguished if we would have peace and blessing. Justification concerns our standing, sanctification our state. The former affects our position, the latter our condition. The first deals with judicial relationship, the second with spiritual fellowship.

We must always remember that they are bestowed together, that is, a complete justification and a commencing sanctification; "where the righteousness of Christ adheres, the grace of Christ inheres"; where the one is imputed, the other is imparted; where the one is reckoned, the other is received. But they must never be confused. The first is the foundation of our peace—"Christ for us." The second is the basis of our purity—"Christ in us." Justification is concerned with acceptance; sanctification with attainment. Sanctification admits of degrees; we may be more or less sanctified. Justification has no degrees, but is complete, perfect, final. "Justified from all things" (Acts 13:39).

W. H. Griffith Thomas, *The Catholic Faith*, pp. 83-85. (The Word "Catholic" in this title does not mean Roman Catholic, but universal.)

Luther's favourite book of the Bible was Galatians. He called it his "Katie" after his wife. Here is an extract from his Galatians Commentary on 5:17 that has helped many thousands:

> Let no man therefore despair if he feels the flesh oftentimes to stir up new battles against the spirit. ... Let him pluck up his heart and comfort himself with these words of Paul: "The flesh lusteth against the spirit," etc., and "These are contrary one to another, so that ye do not those things that ye would." For by these sentences he comforteth them that be tempted. As if he should say: It is impossible for you to follow the guiding of the Spirit in all things without any feeling or hindrance of the flesh; nay, the flesh will resist: and so resist and hinder you that ye cannot do those things that gladly ye would. Here, it shall be enough if ye resist the flesh and fulfil not the lust thereof: that is to say, if ye follow the spirit and not the flesh, which easily is overthrown by impatiency, coveteth to revenge, biteth, grudgeth, hateth God, is angry with him, despaireth, etc. Therefore when a man feeleth this battle of the flesh, let him not be discouraged therewith, but let him resist in the Spirit, and say: I am a sinner, and I feel sin in me, for I have not yet put off the flesh, in which sin dwelleth so long as it liveth; but I will obey the spirit and not the flesh: that is, I will by faith and hope lay hold upon Christ, and by his word I will raise up myself, and being so raised up, I will not fulfil the lust of the flesh.

> It is very profitable for the godly to know this, and to bear it well in mind; for it wonderfully comforteth them when they are tempted. When I was a monk I thought by and by that I was utterly cast away if at any time I felt the concupiscence of the flesh: that is to say, if I felt any evil motion, fleshly lust, wrath, hatred, or envy against my brother. I assayed many ways, I went to confession daily, etc., but it profited me not; for the concupiscence of my flesh did always return, so that I could not rest, but was continually vexed with these thoughts: This or that sin thou hast committed; thou art infected with

envy, with impatiency, and such other sins; therefore thou art entered into this holy order in vain, and all thy good works are unprofitable. If then I had rightly understood these sentences of Paul I should not have so miserably tormented myself, but should have thought and said to myself as now commonly I do: Martin, thou shalt not be utterly without sin, for thou hast yet flesh; thou therefore shalt feel the battle thereof, according to that saying of Paul: "The flesh resisteth the spirit." Despair not therefore, but resist it strongly, and fulfil not the lust thereof.

I remember that Staupitz was wont to say: "I have vowed unto God a thousand times, that I would become a better man; but I never performed that which I vowed. Hereafter I will make no such vow; for I have learned by experience, that I am not able to perform it. Unless therefore God be favourable and merciful unto me for Christ's sake, and grant unto me a blessed and happy hour when I shall depart out of this miserable life, I shall not be able with all my vows and all my good deeds, to stand before him." This was not only a true, but a godly and holy desperation; and this must they all confess both with mouth and heart, which shall be saved. For the godly trust not in their own righteousness, but say with David: "Enter not into judgment with thy servant, for in thy sight shall none that liveth be justified"(Ps. 143:2), and "If thou O Lord shouldest straightly mark iniquities, O Lord who shall stand?" (Ps. 130:3). They look unto Christ their reconciler, who gave his life for their sins. Moreover, they know that the remnant of sin, which is in their flesh, is not laid to their charge, but freely pardoned. Notwithstanding in the meanwhile they fight in the Spirit against the flesh, lest they should fulfil the lust thereof. And although they feel the flesh to rage and rebel against the spirit, yet are they not discouraged, nor think therefore that their state and kind of life, and the works which are done according to their calling, displease God: but they raise up themselves by faith.

Here now is a typical comment from Luther on Justification:

St. Paul teaches everywhere that justification does not result from works but from faith alone, that it does not come in instalments but all at once. For the "testament" comprises everything: justification, salvation, the inheritance, and our most prized possession. Through faith it is enjoyed all at once, in order to make it perfectly clear that no work but faith alone affords such blessings of God as justification and salvation, and that faith makes us children and heirs at once and not in piecemeal manner, as good works must be performed. As children and heirs we then freely perform all manner of good works without anything of that menial spirit which presumes to become pious and meritorious by such service. Merit is unnecessary. Faith gives everything gratuitously, gives more indeed than anyone can merit.

What Luther Says, Vol. 2, p. 2217

Related comments:

"Ah, how large a part of righteousness it is to want to be righteous." "This is the rule, and this must be the verdict: Either go to hell or consider your own righteousness a loss and mere dirt" (*Ibid.*, Vol. 3, pp. 3927, 3929).

Such then was the essence of what Martin Luther learned, and with which he changed the lives ultimately of many millions. This is "the faith that was once for all entrusted to the saints" (Jude 3). Every generation is challenged to recapture and proclaim it.

John Wesley 1703-1791

In the century preceding the Napoleonic wars religion in England seemed extinct. It was truly a post-Christian age. Christianity came near to its death-swoon, says W. H. Fitchett.

It was the Cinderella of the centuries. "Soul extinct, stomach well alive," summarized Carlyle. Every sixth house in London was a gin shop, and gin seemed to have debauched most of London's inhabitants, but not London alone. Open revolt against religion and the churches existed in both extremes of English society. The historian Green tell us that, "the poor were ignorant and brutal to a degree impossible now to realize; the rich linked a foulness of life now happily almost inconceivable." Judges swore on the bench, and naval chaplains during their sermons. The King and his court were profane to such an extent it was as though they had no other vocabulary. Not only parents, but children, were rendered without ability or hope because of drunkenness.

Then came the revolution—not one like that of France with its Reign of Terror, but a revolution in religion and morals. Three men found the gospel and changed their world—John and Charles Wesley and George Whitefield.

Why are religious people in general, even religious leaders, so slow to accept God's good news? Because every man, regardless of his church affiliation, or lack of it, is at heart a Pharisee. He believes he can establish his own righteousness, and that then God will love him. A close study of the diary of John Wesley shows the spiritual pilgrimage of many. Note his biographer's comment:

> He had sat at the feet of many instructors and had read many books. He had been a sacerdotalist, an ascetic, a mystic, a legalist, all in turn—nay, all together! And yet, through all these stages, he had persistently misread the true order of the spiritual world. He believed that a changed life was not the fruit of forgiveness, but its cause. Good works, he held, came before forgiveness and constituted the title to it; they did not come after it and represent its effects. He had, in every mood of his soul missed the great secret of Christianity, lying so near, and level to the intelligence of a child; the secret of a personal salvation, the free gift of God's infinite love through Christ; salvation received through Christ and by faith; a salvation attested by the Spirit of God and verified in the consciousness.

W. H. Fitchett, *Wesley and His Century*, p. 128

What had Fitchett read in Wesley's diary, which revealed the secret of that spiritual giant's original poverty, and ours? Note the following extracts:

> [As a child] I was carefully taught that I could only be saved by universal obedience; by keeping all the commandments of God; in the meaning of which I was diligently instructed … But all that was said to me of inward obedience, or holiness, I neither understood nor remembered. So that I was indeed as ignorant of the true meaning of the law as I was of the gospel of Christ.

> [As a schoolboy] And what I now hoped to be saved by was:

> (1) Not being so bad as other people; (2) having still a kindness for religion; (3) reading the Bible, going to church, and saying my prayers.

[In later years before conversion] And by my continued endeavour to keep his whole law, inward and outward, to the utmost of my power, I was persuaded that I should be accepted of him, and thought I was even then in a state of salvation.

[After failure as a missionary] I was strongly convinced that the cause of my uneasiness was unbelief, and that the gaining of a true, living faith was the "one thing needful" for me. But still I fixed not this faith on its right object; I meant only faith in God, not faith in or through Christ. I knew not that I was wholly devoid of this faith, but only thought I had not enough of it.

Wesley's mother, Susannah, may have been the most capable woman in England, and the prettiest. She was the twenty-fifth child of Dr. Annesley, and after her marriage brought nineteen children of her own into the world. Her husband Samuel did not have his wife's uncommon sense, though there can be no doubting the integrity of his faith and life. Susannah knew Greek, Latin, and French and was able to hold her own in any religious controversy. She possessed multifarious talents and virtues, but she did not know the gospel. As religious as she was, as conscientious as she was, as faithful as she was in even that which was least, she lacked the joy of Christian assurance— because the New Testament gospel was still a sealed book to her. Because a child rarely exceeds the religion of its mother, her famous son toiled in spiritual chains until he was 35 years of age.

When John was only six years old the rectory took fire, perhaps because of unhappy parishioners who thought little of damaging the property of their parson. A tiny face was seen through the window of the upper storey—behind that tiny figure was a wall about to collapse. One farmer stood by the wall of the burning house and invited another to mount his shoulders. So they rescued the endangered lad, and ever afterwards he thought of himself as "a brand plucked from the burning."

At Oxford University, many years later, John became the leading figure of the Holy Club—a group of intelligent, educated, and devout men of the university. They were punctilious in all known duties, prayer, fasting, church services, and ministry to the poor. But one thing they lacked—the gospel.

After his ordination and early service beside his father, Wesley went to America. He wrote in his dairy that he was going there to convert the Indians and then he added, "But who will convert me?" En route a great storm threatened to send his ship to the bottom but a group of Moravian pilgrims sang on, apparently unperturbed. He never forgot the incident, and it encouraged him to fellowship with the Moravians back in England. Through that association (after his absolute failure as a missionary) he found himself one evening listening to a reader of Luther's *Epistle to the Romans*. In his diary Wesley tells us what happened:

> About a quarter before nine, while he was describing the change that God works in the heart through faith in Christ, I felt my heart strangely warmed. I felt I did trust in Christ, Christ alone, for salvation; and an assurance was given me that he had taken away my sins, even mine, and saved me from the law of sin and death."

This was the moment that would result in the transformation of England. According to historian Lecky the event of that hour was more important for England than all her famous victories by land and sea. At approximately the same time his brother Charles was converted, and on meeting they sang a hymn with great joy and parted with prayer.

Often we use the expression "it is too good to be true." But in the case of the gospel "it is so good it must be true." Note this well: what argument cannot accomplish, the Spirit of God can. Millions of Christians can testify that their conversion came by a movement of the Spirit upon them, convincing them of the love of God and the glorious truth that salvation is free. Wesley, the learned reverend minister of the church, who knew not the gospel, received it in a flash from God himself. And so it has been and will continue to be with millions. We cannot hammer a rosebud open, and we cannot argue a person into believing in the love of God. But God can love us into loving him. And that is exactly what he does.

Later, the converted can think on the fact that the good news is such that no one could have invented it. It has to be from God. Who can read the words of Luke 15: "When he (the prodigal) was yet a great way off, his father saw him and had compassion and ran and fell on his neck and kissed him" (verse 20), without sensing that only God could have told that story about such forgiving love. The Bible is self-authenticating to all who have an honest desire to know and do the will of God (John 7:17). As the days go by in the Christian life, the believer is more and more convinced that such a wonderful plan as that of redemption had its origin only in a divine heart.

Marvel at the manner in which the gospel reconciles mercy and justice, and thereby God and man. It would not have been enough for any of us to be merely forgiven. We want to know that our forgiveness is just, that mercy and justice have been reconciled by the intervening act of God on Calvary.

Think how marvellous is the fundamental truth of the Trinity—God over us, God for us, and God in us. The Son executes the Father's plans, but the Spirit applies his saving work to the hungry soul. Then we sense that "only one subject should prevail in Christian conversation, and that it should swallow up every other, for it is the sweetest melody from human lips—Christ our Righteousness." Surely this is the most amazing truth under heaven, that God should devise a plan whereby He might justify the ungodly.

Tell the world: "You don't have to be good to be saved; you have to be saved to be good." "It's not who you are, but whose you are." "Whosoever will may come," and Christ has promised: "Him that comes to me I will in no wise cast out." Who would invent such words as found in Matthew 12:31: "All manner of sin and blasphemy shall be forgiven unto men"?

Wesley went forth from the night meeting at Aldersgate Street to open more tollgates than any man in England. He would travel about 4,000 miles a year (250,000 miles over his lifetime—all by horseback until he reached his seventies). Ultimately his sermons reached the figure of over 44,200. Whitefield's reached 18,000, but his life was over thirty years shorter than Wesley's.

What sort of man was Wesley? He was physically diminutive, but compact and sturdy. He was humble but dignified; supremely intelligent, but bowing with tender regard to every member of the human family. He was a God-intoxicated proclaimer of the good news, and neither threats nor illness, nor the peculiarities of nature could hinder him. He personified faith, hope, and love. All sensed that here was a truly happy man, not swayed by any untoward circumstance, but rejoicing in the benign sovereignty of God his friend. Yet Wesley could write to his brother Charles to say that he did not love God as he should.

He was the best-known figure in the land during the last half of the eighteenth century.

> [He had] a calm intensity of energy, which has been rarely paralleled in any generation. In range, speed, intensity, and effectiveness, Wesley

must always remain one of the greatest workers known to mankind. He seemed to live many lives in one, and each life was of amazing fullness. He preached more sermons, travelled more miles, published more books, wrote more letters, built more churches, waged more controversies, and influenced more lives than any other man in English history. And through it all, as he himself, in a humorous paradox puts it, "he had no time to be in a hurry."

Wesley and His Century, p. 431

He believed his body to be the temple of God, and throughout his long life he studied the laws of health and obeyed them. He almost spanned the eighteenth century. He gave minute health counsels to his associate preachers regarding sleep, exercise, diet, and the like. As with many impressive figures before and after him, he saw advantages in vegetarianism.

Wesley was exactly that "most formidable and terrible of all combinations," a practical mystic. His life thrilled with forces which streamed upon him from spiritual realms; and yet he kept his feet on the solid earth and had the keenest vision for the facts of earth ... No man ever moved more quickly, and none was ever less in a hurry than he. There was something of the inexorable and unhurrying swiftness of a planet about him; and something, too, of its shattering impact. And yet a strange air of repose—the quiet which is born of problems solved and of victory attained—lay upon him....

Wesley had ideals beyond the reach of other men's vision, but absolutely clear to himself. He trod with an assured step; he spoke as one who knew. He was absolutely emptied of selfishness. So he became for those about him, in a sense, an embodied conscience. Here was one human spirit, at least, utterly given up to divine things; one human soul in which religion had fulfilled all its offices. And with all his radiant cheerfulness there was something of the unconscious loftiness of Alpine peaks about him; a remoteness—as though caught from some purer air—from the pursuits and desires of ordinary men. His very face was a rebuke to all mean things....

A sort of perpetual radiance shone in him and streamed from him. ... unclouded cheerfulness. Alexander Knox, who knew Wesley well said, ... "My acquaintance with him has done more to teach me what a heaven upon earth is implied in the maturity of Christian piety than I have elsewhere seen or heard or read." His countenance and conversation expressed an habitual gaiety of heart. Wesley himself declared that, "he had not felt lowness of spirits one quarter of an hour in his life. Ten thousand cares were no more weight to his mind than ten thousand hairs to his head."…

Dr. Johnson, himself a glutton in talk, complained to Patty Wesley of her brother: "I hate to meet John Wesley," he said. "The dog enchants you with his conversation, and then breaks away to go and visit some old woman." …

Once, when tempted to linger in a lovely landscape, Wesley cried, "I believe there is an eternity, I must arise and go hence"; and those words express the temper of his life. He lived in the spirit of Andrew Marvel's strong lines:
"Ever at my back I hear
Time's winged chariots hurrying near."
Wesley and His Century, pp. 431-434

Few men have ever been more systematically generous than Wesley. He lived with the utmost economy himself, and gave away the whole surplus of his income. "When he had thirty pounds a year, he lived on twenty-eight, and gave away two. The next year, receiving sixty pounds, he still lived on twenty-eight, and gave away two-and-thirty. The third year he received ninety pounds, and gave away sixty-two. The fourth year he received a hundred and twenty pounds. Still he lived on twenty-eight, and gave to the poor ninety-two."
Ibid., pp. 436-437

And what did he preach? We quote from a few of his recorded sermons, though the originals were much more lively.

What is justification? … It is not the being made actually just and righteous. That is sanctification; which is, indeed, in some degree, the immediate fruit of justification, but, nevertheless, is a distinct gift from God, and of a totally different nature. The one implies what God does for us through his Son; the other, what he works in us by his Spirit.…

Justification is the clearing us from the accusation brought against us by the law, …

Who are they that are justified? … the ungodly.…

Faith is the necessary condition of justification; yea, and the only necessary condition thereof … the very moment God giveth faith (for it is the gift of God) to the "ungodly" that "worketh not," that "faith is counted to him for righteousness," the very moment he believeth.

"Justification by Faith," *Sermons*, Vol. 1, p. 56 ff.

But in what sense is this righteousness imputed to believers? In this: all believers are forgiven and accepted, not for the sake of anything in them, or of anything that ever was, that is, or ever can be done by them, but wholly and solely for the sake of what Christ hath done and suffered for them. … And this is not only the means of our obtaining the favour of God, but of our continuing therein. It is thus we come to God at first; it is by the same we come unto him ever after. … And this is the doctrine which I have constantly believed and taught, for nearly eight and twenty years. … The righteousness of Christ is imputed to every believer.

"The Lord our Righteousness," *Sermons,* Vol. 1, p. 238 ff.

While justification was Wesley's main theme, he often preached on other topics pertinent to the Christian life. When Fitchett wrote his chapter, "The Secret of the Great Revival," he included these comments upon the matters preached on by Wesley and his helpers:

What are evangelical doctrines? A chain of mountain peaks that pierce to the crown of the heavens, and on whose summits brood perpetual sunshine! They constitute a close-knitted succession of truths that break out of eternity and have its scale—truths that relate to sin, and proclaim its measureless guilt, its hurrying and inevitable doom; but which also reveal an immediate and personal deliverance from sin—a deliverance which comes as an act of divine grace, and on the simplest terms of penitential acceptance. But it is no light and easy deliverance, which costs the Deliverer nothing. It is the supreme miracle of the spiritual universe, made possible only by the mystery of Christ's redemption. It is brought near by the mystery of the Holy Spirit's grace. It sets the forgiven soul in personal and rejoicing relationship with a reconciled and loving Father.

A divine redemption; a realized pardon; a restored relationship to God through faith; the entrance of supernatural forces into the life by the grace of the Divine spirit; the present and perfect attainment of God's ideal in the character. And all this made intelligible and credible by the redeeming work and offices of Jesus Christ—and by the saving energies of the Holy Spirit in the human soul! This is the evangelical version of Christianity!

Ibid., p. 171

George Whitefield. 1714-1770

This man, who preached with only brief intermissions in Britain and America for the most of 40 years, was perhaps the greatest preacher of all time. So say many who have studied his life and work.

As an orator there has scarcely ever been his equal. His voice was not only powerful, but beautifully modulated and under perfect control. … It had a most moving and melting quality that none could resist, and which was the envy of the famous actor David Garrick. … [and] could pull out all the stops of the entire gamut of the human emotions.

Arnold A. Dallimore, *George Whitefield: The Life and Times of the Great Evangelist of the Eighteenth-Century Revival,* Vol. 1, 1970, p. ix

Whitefield was possibly the most loving and lovable proclaimer of grace ever known. He pioneered open-air preaching. "From the age of twenty-two till his death he was the foremost figure of the immense religious movement that held the attention of multitudes on both sides of the Atlantic" (Dallimore). But he wore himself out by the age of 55 after setting on foot influences which would never end. Said Cowper of him:

He followed Paul—his zeal a kindred flame,
His apostolic charity the same.

"Between 1730 and 1740 the life of England was foul with moral corruption and crippled by spiritual decay" (Dallimore), yet it was at such a time that God called forth the Wesley brothers and Whitefield to stir and cleanse the nation. Historian J. R. Green has written of this time:

A religious revival burst forth … which changed in a few years the whole temper of English society. The Church was restored to life and activity. Religion carried to the hearts of the people a fresh spirit of moral zeal, while it purified our literature and our manners. A new philanthropy reformed our prisons, infused clemency and wisdom into our penal laws, abolished the slave trade, and gave the first impulse to popular education.

Cited by Arnold Dallimore, *George Whitefield*, p. 32

Whitefield's ancestry was clerical, educated and cultured, but he himself spent his early years serving in the best-known hostelry in Gloucester as a tapster, cleaning and mopping. His father died at the age of 35, and his mother's later marriage was a failure. The new husband turned out to be a drunkard, and after 6 years the couple separated. These were the most formative years of the life of George. No wonder he fell into the typical vices of youth, but these years were interspersed with devotion to religion. At times he played "church" with himself the preacher. While he stole money from his mother, some of it purchased books of piety, and some of it he gave to the poor. He told his sister that he was convinced God had a special work for him to do.

At St. Mary's school he became acquainted with "a set of debauched, abandoned, atheistical youths and was soon in a fair way of being as infamous as the worst of them."

So says his Journal. But then we read: "Oh, stupendous love! God even here stopped me, when running on in a full career to hell! For, just as I was upon the brink of ruin, he gave me a distaste of their principles and practices. … I began now to be more and more watchful over my thoughts, words, and actions." "From his seventeenth year to his dying day, Whitefield lived among embittered enemies and jealous friends, without a stain on his reputation."

pp. 57-58

At eighteen he went to Oxford as a servitor, one who acted as lackey for several well-to-do students. Here Charles Wesley noted his serious demeanor and invited him to breakfast. This was the beginning of a friendship, which would have tremendous consequences for Whitefield and the world. He joined the Holy Club and was among the foremost in practices of religion and philanthropy.

But God in his providence put in his way a book by Henry Scougal, *The Life of God in the Soul of Man*. It pointed out that true religion was a union of the soul with God and a consequent transformed nature. Whitefield wrote: "I knew I must be born again, or be damned."

Then began a series of austerities that almost killed him. He prayed for hours on the ground, or upon his knees, beneath the great trees of the University, and fasted recurringly. Giving up the eating of fruit, he gave the money to the poor. He chose apparel that was patched and shoes that were scuffed. Soon he was so weak he could hardly ascend the stairs to his room and was forced to tell his kind tutor of his condition. A physician was sent for and he was sentenced to bed-rest for seven weeks. During that time he did not cease to pray for the new birth he now believed to be essential.

God put it into his mind that when Jesus prayed, "I thirst," his sufferings were complete. George cried out again and again, "I thirst," and God came to him in power. He knew that he was now a "new creation," and rejoicing began which never ceased until his death nearly 40 years later. Whenever in later years he returned to Oxford he always sought out the spot where he knew God had come to him in mercy.

Returning to Gloucester in order to save his health, he now spent hours daily on his knees with his English Bible, his Greek New Testament, and the Bible commentary by Matthew Henry before him. Much of what he prayed over, line by line, became indelibly inscribed on his heart and mind for the rest of his life. From this storehouse he constantly drew when later he preached 40 hours per week.

It was falsely reported that at his first sermon he had driven 15 people mad. The presiding Bishop expressed the hope that many more would thus be driven to extremity. Justification by faith and its accompanying new birth was Whitefield's great theme, and multitudes responded.

The very day he set off for Georgia in America in response to a call from the Wesley brothers there, John Wesley returned to England, a broken-hearted failure. Whitefield's congregations wept as he bid them farewell. After a year's ministry in Georgia he returned to England to find the church doors closed against him. So he took to the fields and, at times, 20,000 or more came to listen. He made 14 preaching tours of Scotland, and returned seven times to America. Frequently he delivered 20 sermons in one week.

Whitefield believed in Calvin's predestination, and here he and Wesley differed, but the funeral service Wesley took for George was one of unparalleled affection and respect. Other preachers may have been more learned, but none were more eloquent and moving than this former hostelry tapster who found the gospel of justification by faith and took it to the world.

Charles Spurgeon 1834-1892

If ever there was a parallel to Whitefield in oratorical skills and gospel zeal it was Spurgeon. Even today more people around the world read Spurgeon than any other religious writer. His ministry embraced the world, though he himself rarely travelled further beyond the British Isles than across the English Channel. American newspapers printed his sermons, and multitudes across Europe, Canada, and Australia learned the gospel of justification by faith from the eloquent London preacher.

He founded a Pastor's College, an orphanage, temperance and clothing societies, a Pioneer Mission, and a Colportage Association. During his 38-year London ministry he added to the church almost 15,000 new members.

It is doubtful whether any minister who ever lived (except Calvin) toiled as Spurgeon did. His labours were almost unremitting (though he strove unsuccessfully to preserve a weekly day for a reprieve), and partly responsible for his frequent bouts of illness and early death. There are about 100 books that bear his name as author. Many of these were compiled from his regular preaching.

He was an evangelical Calvinist, but this never hindered his free offers of grace. A bell-like voice, a mastery of language, and his keen sense of humour contributed to his fascination as a preacher. Converted through the ministry of a lay preacher when only 15, he was energized by the gospel to personally present justification by faith to congregations across England, Scotland, Ireland, Wales, and Western Europe. Over several years he averaged 8 to 12 outside services a week, all over the Empire, and Holland and France. His London church so grew that a larger building was needed, and the Metropolitan Tabernacle was completed in 1861.

Through his early years of ministry he faced a tide of slander and vilification, including bitter criticisms by fellow ministers who were jealous of his popularity. In 1865 he preached to approximately 12,000 people in the Surrey Music Hall. Mischief-makers, without conscience, caused a panic by shouting "Fire!" where no fire was. Seven people died in the confusion, and many were seriously injured. Spurgeon's grief almost cost him his reason. Only the unceasing ministry of the Holy Spirit restored him, but he bore the emotional and mental scars till his death. "Giant Despair" became his recurring enemy.

From November 1856 to December 1859 10,000 people crowded the Surrey Hall meetings. London cabbies shouted "Over the river to Charlie." After the Tabernacle was completed, an average of 5,000 people assembled every Sunday, morning and evening. Once a quarter he asked his own people to stay away that others might come. And come they did, jamming the vast Tabernacle. When the Tabernacle was being refurbished in 1867 Spurgeon preached in the Agricultural Hall, Islington with 20,000 in average attendance. The elite came, including Gladstone, Ruskin, Shaftesbury, Queen Victoria along with famous globetrotters, statesmen, soldiers, authors, artists, and industrial captains. Richard Ellsworth Day in his biography (*The Shadow of the Broad Brim*) adds to the list: "rich man, poor man, beggar man, thief; factory girls, artisans, street women, ne'er-do-wells and drunks; farmers, carter's boys, shopkeepers and dairy maids."

But pre-eminently his listeners were the common people. In a letter Spurgeon wrote: "The Lord Mayor, a Jew has been… the Chief Commissioner of Police also … but better still, some thieves, thimbleriggers (a shell game), harlots; … and some are now in the church." By the time of his death Baptists had become a world force.

A well known Doctor of Divinity wrote a pamphlet about Spurgeon in which the following appeared—words addressed first to Spurgeon, and next to every minister:

> You have strong faith, and as the result, intense earnestness. In this lies, as in the hair of Samson, the secret of your power. Go on, my brother, and may God give you a still larger amount of ministerial success! "Preach the Word," the old theology, that "glorious gospel of the blessed God," for which apostles laboured and martyrs died. In all your teachings, continue to exhibit the Cross of Christ as occupying, in the Christian revelation, like the sun in our planetary system, the very centre, and imparting to all their light and heat. Tell the people that every doctrine, duty, or promise of the

Scriptures stands intimately connected with the Cross, and from that connection derives its meaning and value to us. Thus exhibiting the whole system of Divine Truth in its harmony and symmetry, what a glorious prospect of honour, happiness, and usefulness presents itself to your view!

W. Joseph Harrald, *The Autobiography of Charles H. Spurgeon: 1854-1860*, p. 79

Here are some fragments from his preaching:

My Lord wore my crown of thorns for me, why should I wear it too? He took our griefs and carried our sorrows that we might be a happy people and be able to obey the command, "Take no thought for the morrow." Ours is the crown of loving kindness and tender mercies, and we wear it when we cast all our care on him who careth for us. Take but a thorn out of this crown and use it as a lancet and it will let out the hot blood of passion and abate the fever of pride. It is a wonderful remedy for swelling flesh and grievous boils of sin. He who sees Jesus crowned with thorns will loathe to look upon self, except it be though tears of contrition.

No evil can happen to me, seeming ill is but another form of benediction. If all events shall aid me, what matters in what dress they come, whether of scarlet and fine linen, or sackcloth and ashes. … the bitter is sweet and medicine is food. Courage, ye shall meet nought but friends between this and the pearly gates, or if you meet an enemy it will be a conquered one … the winds which toss the waves of the Atlantic of your life are all sure to waft your ship safely into the desired haven. Every wind that rises, whether soft or fierce, is a divine monsoon hurrying in the same direction as your soul's desires. … God walks in the tempest and rules the storm.

Spurgeon's first words at the Tabernacle were these:

I would propose that the subject of the Ministry in this house, as long as this platform shall stand, and as long as this house shall be frequented by worshippers, shall be the person of Jesus Christ. I am never ashamed to avow myself a Calvinist; I do not hesitate to take the name of Baptist; but if I am asked what is my creed, I reply, "It is Jesus Christ." My venerated predecessor, Dr. Gill, has left a

> Body of Divinity, admirable and excellent in its way; but the Body of Divinity to which I would pin and bind myself for ever, God helping me, is not his system, or any other human treatise; but Christ Jesus, who is the sum and substance of the gospel, who is in himself all theology, the incarnation of every precious truth, the all-glorious personal embodiment of the way, the truth, and the life.

And now his last words just before his death:

> If you wear the livery of Christ, you will find him so meek and lowly of heart that you will find rest unto your souls. He is the most magnanimous of captains. There never was his like among the choicest of princes. He is always to be found in the thickest part of the battle. When the wind blows cold he always takes the bleak side of the hill. The heaviest end of the Cross lies ever on his shoulders. If he bids us carry a burden, he carries it also. If there is anything that is gracious, generous, kind, and tender, yea, lavish and superabundant in love, you will always find it in him. His service is life, peace, joy. Oh, that you would enter on it at once! God help you to enlist under the banner of Jesus Christ.

Recommended is the two-volume autobiography *The Early Years* (Volume 1); and *The Full Harvest* (Volume 2).

Catherine Booth (1829-1890)

She was smarter than her husband, and most ministers, contemporary or subsequent. Yet she suffered physical pain most of her life, and particularly in her last years when suffering from cancer. But she was a great and shining light and an inspiration to countless thousands. The passage of time has not dimmed that luminescence but increased it, as the story of her sacrificial and loving ministry has spread around the world. She was one of the greatest of women preachers and drew large appreciative crowds.

When her husband's governing body legislated that he should not preach beyond certain geographical boundaries, Catherine stood and, in a voice that could be heard by all in the great hall, exclaimed: "No! Never!" Then she and her husband walked out of the assembly, and not long later originated the Salvation Army. Long before this she had said to the man who was to be her husband: "We will make our home the brightest spot on earth, and we will be to each other kind, thoughtful, affectionate, patient, and forbearing—yes, we will." And so it was. Even when disturbed William came home in an emotional storm, he was always nothing but gentle and loving to his Catherine. When told she would die of her breast cancer she exclaimed: "O, that means I will not be able to nurse William in his last days." Theirs was a true love match all their days. The General never remarried.

Catherine was a Christian feminist and would not tolerate speech or action that attempted to downgrade her sex. With meticulous care she studied Scripture on the role of women and often preached on that topic. See her sermon: "Female Ministry; or, Woman's Right to Preach the Gospel" in her book *Practical Religion*. She deals with all texts that supposedly forbid a woman to speak in the church and then says:

> Notwithstanding, however, all this opposition to female ministry on the part of those deemed authorities in the Church, there have been some in all ages in whom the Holy Ghost has wrought so mightily, that at the sacrifice of reputation and all things most dear, they have been compelled to come out as witnesses for Jesus and ambassadors of his gospel. As a rule, these women have been amongst the most devoted and self-denying of the Lord's people, giving indisputable evidence by the purity and beauty of their lives, that they were led by the Spirit of God. Now, if the Word of God forbids female ministry, we would ask how it happens that so many of the most devoted handmaidens of the Lord have felt themselves constrained by the Holy Ghost to exercise it? Surely there must be some mistake somewhere, for the word and the Spirit cannot contradict each other. Either the word does not condemn women preaching, or these professedly holy women have been deceived. Will any one venture to assert that such women as Mrs. Elizabeth Fry, Mrs. Fletcher of Madeley, and Mrs. Smith, have been deceived with respect to their call to deliver the Gospel messages to their fellow-creatures? If not, then God does call and qualify women to preach, and his word, rightly understood, cannot forbid what his Spirit enjoins.

> Further, it is a significant fact, which we commend to the consideration of all thoughtful Christians, that the public ministry of women has been eminently owned of God in the salvation of souls and the edification of his people.

pp. 160-161

General Booth spoke at his wife's graveside. Here are some of his words:

> If you had a tree under your window, which for forty years had been your shadow from the burning sun, whose flowers had been the adornment and beauty of your life, whose fruit had been almost the very stay of your existence.…

> If you had a servant who, for all this long time, had served you without fee or reward, who had ministered, for very love, to your health and comfort.…

> If you had a counsellor who in hours—continually occurring—of perplexity and amazement, had ever advised you.…

> If you had a friend who had understood your very nature, the rise and fall of your feelings, the bent of your thoughts, and the purpose of your existence; a friend whose communion had ever been pleasant— the most pleasant of all other friends, to whom you had ever turned with satisfaction.…

> If you had had a mother of your children who had cradled and nursed and trained them for the service of the living God, in which you most delighted; a mother indeed.…

> If you had a wife, a sweet love of a wife, who for 40 years had never given you real cause for grief; a wife who had stood with you side by side in the battle's front, who had been a comrade to you, ever willing to interpose herself between you and the enemy and ever the strongest when the battle was fiercest.…

> My comrades, roll all these qualities into one personality and what would be lost in each I have lost, all in one. There has been taken away from me the delight of my eyes, the inspiration of my soul.… yet, my comrades, my heart is full of gratitude … that the long valley of the shadow of death has been trodden … gratitude because God lent me for so long a season such a treasure. I have been thinking, if I had to point out her three qualities to you here, they would be: first, she was good. She was washed in the Blood of the Lamb. To the last moment her cry was, "A sinner saved by grace."

She was a thorough hater of shams, hypocrisies, and make-believes. Second, she was love. Her whole soul was full of tender, deep compassion. I was thinking this morning that she suffered more in her lifetime through her compassion for poor dumb animals than some suffer for the wide, wide world of sinning, sorrowing mortals! Oh, how she loved, how she compassioned, how she pitied.… How she longed to put her arms round the sorrowful and help them! Lastly she was a warrior. She liked the fight. She was not one who said to others, " Go!" but, "Here, let me go!"

I have never turned from her these 40 years for any journeyings on my mission of mercy, but I have longed to get back, and have counted the weeks, days, and hours, which should take me again to her side. And now she has gone away for the last time. What, then, is there left for me to do … when I have served my Christ and my generation according to the will of God—which I vow this afternoon I will, to the last drop of my blood—then I trust that she will bid me welcome to the skies as God bade her. God bless you all, Amen.

Hannah Whitall Smith (1832-1911)

Millions have thanked God for the ministry by pen and voice of this Quaker lady who sowed the seed for the Keswick Conventions. She testified to a life of spiritual victory and rest through complete commitment to Christ. Though herself an "amazing beauty," her real wealth lay in her possession of Christ and her understanding of how the gospel should govern everyday life.

The "faith" referred to in the phrase, "justification by faith," means "total confidence." This is the theme of her great book *The Christian's Secret of a Happy Life*, which has been translated into many languages, and gone through many editions, and which is still in print comforting and inspiring countless thousands. It is simply and plainly written so that a child can understand it, but its message is the practical outworking of the Christian gospel.

Here is a representative quotation from her chief book:

> What is needed, then, is to see God in everything, and to receive everything directly from his hands, with no intervention of second causes; and it is to just this that we must be brought before we can know an abiding experience of entire abandonment and perfect trust.

Our abandonment must be to God, not to man, and our trust must be in him, not in any arm of flesh, or we shall fall at the first trial.

The question here confronts us at once, "But is God in everything, and have we any warrant from the Scriptures for receiving everything from his hands without regarding the second causes that may have been instrumental in bringing them about?" I answer to this, unhesitatingly, Yes to the children of God, everything comes directly from their Father's hand. No matter who or what may have been the apparent agents. There are no "second causes" for them.

The whole teaching of Scripture asserts and implies this. Not a sparrow falls to the ground without our Father. The very hairs of our head are all numbered. We are not to be careful about anything, because our Father cares for us. We are not to avenge ourselves, because our Father has charged himself with our defense. We are not to fear, for the Lord is on our side. No one can be against us, because he is for us. We shall not want, for He is our Shepherd. When we pass through the rivers they shall not overflow us, and when we walk through the fire we shall not be burned, because he will be with us. He shuts the mouths of lions, that they cannot hurt us. "He delivereth and rescueth." "He changes the times and the seasons; he removeth kings and setteth up kings." A man's heart is in his hand. And, "as the rivers of water, he turneth it whithersoever he will." He ruleth over the kingdoms of the heathen; and in his hand there is power and might, "so that none is able to withstand" him. "He ruleth the raging of the sea; when the waves thereof arise, he stilleth them." He "bringeth the counsel of the heathen to naught; he maketh the devices of the people of none effect." "Whatsoever the Lord pleaseth, that doeth he, in heaven and in earth, in the seas and all deep places." "Lo, these are parts of his ways; but how little a portion is heard of him? But the thunder of his power who can understand?" "Hast thou not known? Hast thou not heard, that the everlasting God, the Lord, the Creator of the ends of the earth, fainteth not, neither is weary? There is no searching of his understanding."

And it is this very God who is declared to be "our refuge and strength, a very present help in trouble. Therefore will we not fear, though the earth be removed, and though the mountains be carried into the midst of the sea; though the waters thereof roar and be troubled, though the mountains shake with the swelling thereof." "I will say of the Lord, he is my refuge and my fortress; my God; in him will I trust...."

To my own mind, these Scriptures, and many others like them, settle forever the question as to the power of "second causes" in the life of the children of God. Second causes must all be under the control of our Father, and not one of them can touch us except with his knowledge and by his permission. It may be the sin of man that originates the action, and therefore the thing itself cannot be said to be the will of God, but by the time it reaches us it has become God's will for us, and must be accepted as directly from his hands. No man or company of men, no power in earth or heaven, can touch that soul which is abiding in Christ, without passing first through his encircling presence, and receiving the seal of his permission. If God be for us, it matters not who may be against us; nothing can disturb us or harm us, except he shall see that it is best for us, and shall stand aside to let it pass....

He ... takes note of the minutest matters that can affect the lives of his children, and regulates them all according to his own perfect will, let their origin be what they may.

The Christian's Secret of a Happy Life, pp. 102-104

In addition to the many Scriptures quoted by Hannah Whitall Smith, the reader should closely study Luke 21:16-18—every word of it, particularly the apparent, but not real contradiction between "some of you they shall cause to be put to death," and "But there shall not a hair of your head perish." See also Genesis 50:20; and 45:5, which alone are sufficient to prove Hannah's case and give us peace.

Chapter 15

Conclusion

We now offer a summary of what has been set out in these chapters. The objective historic apostolic gospel is to be proclaimed to all the world with Pentecostal power (Matthew 24:14; Mark 13:10; Revelation 10:1-3; 14:5; and 18:1-4). This will be the equivalent, but on a worldwide scale, of Christ's proclamation by his Triumphal Entry into Jerusalem at the beginning of Passion Week. That event polarized his world and led to a death decree against him, the execution of which was preceded by a terrible time of tribulation. Judas precipitates the last crisis by his apostasy. He is the Antichrist of that time.

So the final gospel warning will polarize the world. The gospel believers will be looked upon as troublemakers leading to world unrest. Ultimately apostate religion (following the example of Judas) and the state will unite as the final Antichrist to sentence the gospel believers to death. As the majority of earth's inhabitants reject the gospel, the Holy Spirit gradually ceases his pleading with hearts, and his common grace over the unconverted will also ebb away. This removal of the Spirit's influence unleashes all the pent up evil of rebellious human hearts, and the worst tribulation in all of history will begin.

When the world commits the unpardonable sin by sentencing the saints en masse to death, Christ's heavenly ministry ceases, and the seven last plagues begin to fall. Armageddon now reaches its climax as satanic hosts make war on the people of God. The appearance of Christ in the eastern heavens brings consternation to the wicked, who will then blame each other for their troubles and turn violently upon one another. The remnant of the lost are slain by the brightness of Christ's approach, but simultaneously the righteous dead, including the recent martyrs, will rise from their graves to meet their Lord.

All this may sound fantastic to some, but who would have believed a novel written in the early 1930s describing both a terrible European holocaust and a dreadful atomic weapon that would fill the later decades with horror? The present world seems poised now close to catastrophe, and politicians seem powerless. The existing tendency to riot and protest in the most civilized countries of the world are a shadow of things to come. Already over a billion people are close to starvation. What will happen if and when that number is tripled?

The challenge for believers is to place their confidence in the everlasting gospel and the Lord who is its centre. We are to emulate Daniel concerning whom no fault could be found except concerning the law of his God. The Apostles after Pentecost prefigure the last generation of saints who will fear neither perils nor murderous opponents.

In *The Brothers Karamazov*, Dostoyevsky wrote his creed:

> I believe like a child that suffering will be healed and made up for, that all the humiliating absurdity of human contradictions will vanish like a pitiful mirage, like the despicable fabrication of the impotent and infinitely small Euclidean mind of man, that in the world's finale, at the moment of eternal harmony, something so precious will come to pass that it will suffice for all hearts, for the comforting of all resentments, for the atonement of all the crimes of humanity, of all the blood that they've shed; that it will make it not only possible to forgive but to justify all that has happened.

We cannot but be touched by such words, but even more glorious are those found at the close of Scripture:

> Now the dwelling of God is with men, and he will live with them. They will be his people, and God himself will be their God. He will wipe every tear from their eyes. There will be no more death or mourning or crying or pain, for the old order of things has passed away. I am making everything new.

Glossary

Abomination: in the Old Testament an idol or something associated with idolatrous worship.

Abomination of Desolation: a title found in apocalyptic works for Antichrist. It means a power or person that is idolatrous and persecuting.

Anarthrous: used without the article—i.e. without "the."

Antichrist: a genus including all who counterfeit or oppose Christ and his truth. Not necessarily just a single individual.

Antinomianism: the false belief that the Law of God is no longer binding on believers.

Apocalyptic: type of literature characterized by bizarre imagery symbolizing the future. The prophetic chapters of Daniel and Revelation are in this category.

Apocrypha: collection of uninspired Jewish writings between the time of Malachi and Christ—included in the Douay Version of the Bible but usually not in Protestant versions.

Apostasy: a falling away from truth.

Apotelesmatic: recurring fulfilments of prophetic forecasts. For example, Matthew 24 points to the destruction of Jerusalem, but also to the end of the world.

Armageddon: a symbolic name for the last conflict between good and evil.

Article: equals "the."

Babylon: in the New Testament a symbolic name for apostate religion.

Bête noire: black beast, fearful entity.

Consensus: agreement.

Corpus: a complete collection of writings.

Diabolus: the devil.

Eschatological: pertaining to the last times.

Euphrates: in Revelation a symbolic name for an invading flood of wicked apostates. The boundary between the church and the world.

Exegesis: investigation of the meaning of Scripture. The result of such investigation.

Expiation: the wiping away of guilt by sacrifice.

Firmament: sky.

Gestalt: an organized whole in which each individual part affects every other.

Genus: group.

Gospel: the good news that because of Christ's substitutionary and representative death all penitents are welcome back to the heart of God and reckoned righteous without any works of their own. The result is always a life dedicated to Christ.

Hermeneutics: principles of interpretation.

Humanism: system of thought that is man-centered and limited to merely human interests.

Imputation: God's gracious attributing of righteousness to the penitent sinner.

Investigative Judgment: theory that in 1844 Christ began a review of the lives of professed believers. Not taken seriously by scholars of any hue.

Justification: God's declaring righteous penitent sinners who believe the gospel.

Legalism: seeking acceptance with God by our good behaviour.

Lexicography: study of dictionaries of foreign languages.

LXX: The Greek translation of the Hebrew Old Testament begun by Jews in the third century B.C.

Millennium: a thousand-year period mentioned in Revelation 20.

Moral Influence Theory: the theory that Christ's death was not a sacrifice but merely a divine gesture to tell of God's love.

New Perspective on Paul: a recent theory that denies the traditional understanding of Paul regarding Justification and holding that Paul's statements against what has been understood as legalism are really only against the "boundary markers" of Jews—holy days, circumcision, food laws. There is no complete homogeneity of belief among those who espouse the New Perspective. Often one scholar rejects the specific interpretation of another.

Passion Week: the last seven days of Christ's time on earth before his resurrection. "Passion" comes from a root meaning "suffering."

Pelagianism: the theory that by our own power we can overcome sin.

Perfectionism: the theory that in this life it is possible to live without sin and sinning.

Pogrom: an organized massacre of the Jews.

Postmillennial: Christ's return and God's kingdom on earth to be set up after a thousand years of peace on this planet.

Predestination: the word is not found in Scripture though predestine (God's planning beforehand) is in the Epistles to the Romans and to the Ephesians. The noun signifies a false theory popularised by Augustine and Calvin that it was God's intention to allocate most human beings to hell and a tiny number to heaven.

Premillennial: Christ's visible return for his people before the millennium.

Prescience: foreknowledge.

Propitiation: the sacrificial means by which sin is forgiven and God's antagonism to evil removed. In the Scriptures it does not have the pagan meaning of "bribing" a reluctant deity.

Prototype: the original, or first of a series.

Pseudepigrapha: Jewish writings ascribed to great characters of the past. Belonging mainly but not solely to documents written in the last centuries before Christ.

Qumran: place by the Dead Sea where the famous Dead Sea biblical scrolls were discovered.

Rectory: parsonage, the home of the local minister.

Sacerdotalism: a form of religion that revolves around priests.

Secularism: the doctrine that human interests should be limited to this present life.

Semipelagianism: the belief that sin is overcome chiefly by our own effort.

Semitic: linked to descendants of Shem, particularly those who used Aramaic or related languages.

Soteriology: the doctrine of salvation. Its ramifications.

Weltanschauung: [German] world-view; philosophy of life.

Yahweh: another form of Jehovah, the Jewish and biblical name for God.

Bibliography

Alexander, Philip S. "Torah and Salvation in Tannaitic Literature," in D. A. Carson, Peter T. O'Brien, and Mark A. Seifrid (eds.), *Justification and Variegated Nomism*, Vol. 1, *The Complexities of Second Temple Judaism*, Tübingen, Mohr Siebeck, 2001, pp. 261-301.

Baldwin, Joyce G. *Daniel*, Leicester, Inter-Varsity Press, 1978.

Barnett, Paul *Romans*, Fearn, Scotland, 2003.

Barrett, C. K. "Paul and the Introspective Conscience," in W. P. Stephens (ed.) *The Bible, the Reformation, and the Church: Essays in Honour of James Atkinson*, Sheffield: Sheffield Academic Press, 1995, pp. 36-48.

Bernard, T. D. *The Progress of Doctrine in the New Testament*, London, Macmillan & Co., 1864.

Blocher, Henri. "Justification of the Ungodly (Sola Fide): Theological Reflections," in D. A. Carson, Peter T. O'Brien, and Mark A. Seifrid (eds.), *Justification and Variegated Nomism*, Vol. 2, *The Paradoxes of Paul*, Tübingen, Mohr-Siebeck, 2004, pp. 465-500.

Boutflower, C. *In and Around the Book of Daniel*, London, S.P.C.K., 1923.

Bruce, F. F. *Romans*, Grand Rapids, Eerdmans, 1963.

Buchanan, James. *The Doctrine of Justification*, London, Banner of Truth Trust, 1961.

Carnell, Edward J. *The Case for Orthodox Theology*, Philadelphia, Westminster Press, 1859.

D.A. Carson, Peter T. O'Brien, and Mark A. Seifrid (eds.), *Justification and Variegated Nomism*, Vol.1, *The Complexities of Second Temple Judaism*, Tübingen, Mohr-Siebeck, 2001.

D.A. Carson, Peter T. O'Brien, and Mark A. Seifrid (eds.), *Justification and Variegated Nomism*, Vol. 2, *The Paradoxes of Paul*, Tübingen, Mohr-Siebeck, 2004.

Chemnitz, Martin *Examination of the Council of Trent*, Part 1, St. Louis, Missouri, Concordia Publishing House, 1971.

Church, R.W. *Pascal and Other Sermons*, Macmillan, London, 1909.

Cullmann, O. *Christ and Time: The Primitive Christian Conception of Time and History*, London, S.C.M. Press, 1951.

Dale, R. W. *The Atonement*, London, Congregational Union of England and Wales, 1899.

Dahl, Nils Alstrup. *Studies in Paul: Theology for the Early Christian Mission*, ed. Minneapolis, Augsburg, 1977.

Denney, James *The Death of Christ*, London, Hodder and Stoughton, 1903.

Denney, James "The Epistles to the Thessalonians," *Expositor's Bible*, London, London, Hodder and Stoughton, 1892.

Dunn, James, D.G. *Jesus, Paul, and the Law: Studies in Mark and Galatians*, Louisville, Westminster/John Knox, 1990.

"Romans 1-8", *Word Biblical Commentary*. 38A, Dallas, Word Press, 1988.

Espy, John M. "Paul's 'Robust Conscience' Re-examined," *New Testament Studies*, Vol. 31, 1985, pp. 161-88.

Everson, Philip H. *The Great Exchange: Justification by Faith Alone*—In the Light of Recent Thought, Leominster, DayOne Publications, 1996.

Farrar, F. W. *History of Interpretation*, London, Macmillan, 1886.

Farrar, F. W. *Life and Work of St. Paul*, London, E.P. Dutton & Co., 1880.

Fitchett, W. H. *Wesley and His Century,* New York, Abingdon Press, 1917.

Ford, Desmond *Crisis, A Commentary on the Book of Revelation,* Vols. 1 & 2, Newcastle, CA, Desmond Ford Publications, 1982.

Ford, Desmond *Daniel and the Coming King,* Newcastle, CA, Desmond Ford Publications, 1996.

Ford, Desmond *For the Sake of the Gospel: Throw Out the Bathwater, But Keep the Baby,* New York, iUniverse, 2008.

Ford, Desmond *In the Heart of Daniel,* New York, iUniverse, 2008.

Ford, Desmond *Jesus Only: What Christ's Living and Dying Mean for You,* New York, iUniverse, 2008.

Ford, Desmond *The Abomination of Desolation in Biblical Eschatology,* University Press of America, Washington D.C., 1979.

Frame, J. E. *A Critical and Exegetical Commentary on the Epistles of St. Paul to the Thessalonians* (ICC), Edinburgh, Scribner, 1912.

Gathercole, S. J. *Where is Boasting? Early Jewish Eschatology and Paul's Response in Romans 1-5,* Grand Rapids, Eerdmans, 2002.

Gathercole, S. J. "Justified by Faith, Justified by his Blood: The Evidence of Romans 3:21-4:25," in D.A. Carson, Peter O'Brien, and Mark A. Seifrid (eds.) *Justification and Variegated Nomism,* Vol. 2, Tubingen, Mohr-Siebeck, 2004, pp. 147-84.

Gathercole, S. J. "What Did Paul Really Mean?" *Christianity Today,* Vol. 51, No. 8, August 2007.

Godet, F. L. *Paul's Epistles to the Romans,* Grand Rapids, Kregel, 1977.

Goldingay, John E. *Daniel,* Word Biblical Commentary, Vol. 30, Dallas, Thomas Nelson, 1989.

Green, Peter *Studies in the Cross,* London, Wells Gardner Darton, 1914.

Habershon, Ada R. *The Study of the Types*, Grand Rapids, Kregel, 1957.

Harrold, W. Joseph (ed.) *The Autobiography of Charles H. Spurgeon: 1854-1860,* New York, F. H. Revell, 1899, p. 79.

Heaton, Eric *Daniel,* Norwich, SCM Press, 1967, p. 195.

Herberg, Will *Protestant, Catholic, Jew: An Essay in American Religious Sociology,* Chicago, UCP, 1955.

Jeffrey, Steve, Ovey, Michael & Sach Andrew *Pierced for Our Transgressions*: rediscovering the glory of penal substitution, Wheaton, IVP, 2007.

Jeremias, J., Hooke, S. H. *The Parables of Jesus*, New York, Scribner, 1954.

Johnson, Gary L. W.; Waters, Guy P. By Faith Alone. Wheaton, 2006.

Keil, Carl Friedrich & Delitzsch, F. *Biblical Commentary on the Book of Daniel: Commentary on the Old Testament*, (trans.) M.G. Easton, Grand Rapids, Eerdmans, 1975.

Kennedy, H. A. A. *St. Paul's Conception of the Last Things*, 2nd ed., Hodder & Stoughton, London, 1904.

Köberle, Adolf *The Quest for Holiness: A Biblical, Historical and Systematic Investigation*, Minneapolis, Augsburg Publishing House, 1936.

Lacoque, A. *The Book of Daniel,* Atlanta, Knox Press, 1979.

Ladd, G. E. "Unity and Variety in New Testament Faith," *Christianity Today*, Vol. 10, Nov. 19, 1965, pp. 21-24.

Laato, Timo *Paul and Judaism: An Anthropological Approach*, Atlanta, Scholars Press, 1995.

Lattey, C. *The Book of Daniel,* Dublin, The Catholic Biblical Association, 1948.

Leupold, H. C. *Exposition of Daniel*, Ohio, Wartburg Press, 1949.

Luther, Martin *Lectures on Galatians, 1535*, in *Luther's Works*, Vol. 26-27, ed. by Jaroslav Pelikan, Saint Louis, Concordia, 1963-64.

Milligan, G. *St. Paul's Epistles to the Thessalonians*, Macmillan, London, 1908.

Milligan, G. "The Book of Revelation," *Expositor's Bible*, London, Hodder & Stoughton, 1889.

Milligan, G. *Lectures on the Apocalypse*, Macmillan, London, 1892.

Minear, P. *I Saw a New Earth*, Washington D.C., Corpus Books, 1968.

Minear, P. "The Wounded Beast", *JBL*, Vol. 72, 1953, pp. 93-101.

Moo, Douglas J. *The Epistle to the Romans, ICC,* Grand Rapids, Wm. B. Eerdmans, 1996.

Morris, L. *The Apostolic Preaching of the Cross*, London, 1955.

Morris, L. *The Cross in the New Testament,* Grand Rapids: Eerdmans, 1965

Moule, C. F. D. "Obligation in the Ethic of Paul," in *Christian History and Interpretation: Studies Presented to John Knox,* eds. W.R. Farmer, C.F.D. Moule & R.R. Niebuhr, Cambridge: Cambridge University Press, 1967, pp. 389-406.

Nineham, D. E. *The Gospel of Saint Mark,* Pelican New Testament Commentaries, London, Penguin Books, 1963.

Orchard, J. B. "Thessalonians and the Synoptic Gospels," *Biblica,* Vol. 19, 1938, pp. 19-42.

Orr, James *The Progress of Dogma*, London, James Clarke, 1901.

Pease, Norval *By Faith Alone,* Mountain View, CA, Pacific Press, 1962.

Pierson, A. T. *God's Living Oracles,* London, Baker & Taylor, 1903.

Pink, Arthur W. *The Atonement*, Swengel, PA, Bible Truth Depot, 1958.

Riggenbach, C. J. "Thessalonians". *Lange's Commentary on the Holy Scriptures,* Edinburgh, T. & T. Clarke, 1868, Vol. 11, pp. 1-163.

Sanders, E. P. *Paul and Palestinian Judaism,* Philadelphia, Fortress, 1977.

Schrenk, Gottlog, Kittel, G. (ed.) "Dikaiow," *Theological Dictionary of the New Testament*, Grand Rapids, Eerdmans, 1964, Vol. 2, pp. 211-19.

Seifrid, Mark A. *Justification by Faith: The Origin and Development of a Central Pauline Theme*, Leiden, Brill, 1992.

Silva, Moises *Philippians,* Grand Rapids, Baker, 1992.

Smith, Wilbur *Therefore Stand*, Boston, W.A. Wilde, 1945.

Stalker, James *The Life of St. Paul*, Edinburgh, T. & T. Clarke, 1885.

Stendahl, Krister *Paul Among Jews and Gentiles* New Haven. Yale University Press, 1994.

Stuhlmacher, Peter *Revisiting Paul's Doctrine of Justification: A Challenge to the New Perspective,* with an essay by Donald A. Hagner. Downers Grove IL, InterVarsity Press, 2001.

Thielman, Frank *From Plight to Solution: A Jewish Framework for Understanding Paul's View of the Law in Galatians and Romans*, Leiden, Brill, 1989.

Thomas, W. H. Griffith *The Catholic Faith*, Hodder & Stoughton, London, 1905.

Torrey, C. C. *Documents of the Primitive Church,* New York, London, Harper & Bros., 1941.

Trueblood, David Elton *Philosophy of Religion,* New York & London, Evanston, 1957.

Westerholm, Stephen *Perspectives Old and New on Paul*, Grand Rapids, Eerdmans, 2004.

Whale, J. S. *Victor and Victim*, Cambridge, 1960.

Whale, J. S. *The Protestant Tradition*, Cambridge, 1962.

White E. G. *The Great Controversy*, Mountain View, CA, Pacific Press, 1950.

White E. G. *Patriarchs and Prophets*, Mountain View, CA, Pacific Press, 1958.

Witherington III, Ben *The Indelible Image*, Downer's Grover, IL, InterVarsity Press, 2009.

Wordsworth, Christopher *Commentary on the Holy Bible*, Cambridge, Rivingtons, 1875.

Wright, N. T. *What Paul Really Said: Was Paul of Tarsus the Real Founder of Christianity?*, Grand Rapids, Eerdmans, 1997.

Young, Edward J. *The Prophecy of Daniel,* Grand Rapids, Eerdmans, 1949.

Young, Norman H. "Who's Cursed—and Why? (Galatians 3:10-14)," *Journal of Biblical Literature*, Vol. 117, 1998, pp. 79-92.

Young, Norman H. "Pronomial Shifts in Paul's Argument to the Galatians," in (eds.) T.W. Hilliard, R.A. Kearsley, C.E. V. Nixon, and A.M. Noble, *Ancient History in a Modern University*, vol.2: *Early Christianity, Late Antiquity, and Beyond*, 1998, Grand Rapids, Eerdmans, pp. 205-15.